MEET THE LUNATICS
WHO RUN YOUR KIDS'
SPORTS LEAGUES

A COACH DAD'S TAKE
ON THE WACKY WORLD
OF YOUTH SPORTS

JACK MALLEY

JRC Publishing
Ridgefield, CT

Illustrations by Dan Berger

Art Design and Concepts by Jack Malley

Cover Design by Dan Berger

Edited by Georgia Stasinos Laudani

This book is dedicated to
Joe, Ryan and Caroline,
who have given me more joy than I
could have ever hoped for in life.

TABLE OF CONTENTS

INTRODUCTION

How did this even happen? One minute I was potty training my 3 year old, in control of the situation, and the next thing I knew, my kid was 6 and I was a small pebble being pushed and pulled by the undertow of the kids sports machine in my town. The people in charge seemed as if they had been studying this stuff for years or maybe even went to some kids sports training school or something. You had the Bobby Knight wannabe dads who insisted on coaching their kids every season. You had the team moms who rigidly enforced inane rules about snack breaks, proper hydration, and mandatory cup wearing. You had the town snobs who looked down their noses at you when you couldn't cough up major chunks of cash for trips by "travel teams." I just couldn't figure out why these adults were taking sporting events played by small children so seriously. More importantly, I wanted to know how the hell they became the bosses of me.

Then, as I actually began to focus on the games my son was playing, so many questions came to mind, such as:

Is it possible that the best shortstop on most every team just happens to be the head coach's son?

Why does the assistant coach's kid play first base even though he has hands of stone?

Is it just a coincidence that the league president's team has the best players?

However, when I thought about it for a while, I recalled that it was the same way when I was a kid – the dads who run the leagues stack their teams with the best athletes and play their kids exclusively at the "star" positions. This doesn't go on for just one season, hell no. It goes on season after season, year after year. The same dads doggedly secure their kids' place in the sun at the expense of all the others.

Remembering these cold hard facts, I decided that I'd had enough of my outsider status and I joined the machine as an assistant coach. Initially, I was looked at with suspicion. But after a while I was accepted, and I began to understand what made the "bosses of me" tick.

In fact, I began to exhibit some of the very same behavior that I ridiculed only months before. I started wearing "coach" type attire, like sweat pants and team t-shirts around town. I began to develop a troublesome antagonism toward the small children that my teams competed against. And I found myself engaged in extended conversations with other parents about such riveting topics as whether little Jimmy or little Bobby is a better "big game" player, the best training methods for 11 year old hoopsters, and whether cleats or sneakers would provide the best traction for 4 year old soccer players.

As I moved along this path, there wasn't really any time for reflection or self-analysis. I mean, I had (in my simple mind) an important job to do as coach, one that required focus and commitment. But after a few seasons of coaching children, I had to take a step back and ask myself whether I was turning into one of the obnoxious, obsessed, over the top parents that I had mocked before I joined up.

There was no doubt that I'd been devoting an inordinate amount of time and energy to my kids' teams and the whole youth sports scene in my town. It was also clear that I had made some questionable decisions, such as talking my 11 year old son into 6:00 am basketball workouts with me before I went to work, and forcing my 6 year old son to play three sports in one spring season, baseball, soccer and lacrosse. On the other hand, I had not yet become a complete embarrassment like the nut cases who scream at umpires and quote Bobby Knight, a lunatic who nobody should emulate.

In order to determine whether I had gone too far, I began a period of in depth analysis of the kids sports scene, a scene that I have been a part of for much of my 51 years. You see, I grew up in a sports obsessed family. My father lived and died with the Brooklyn Dodgers his entire childhood and idolized Pee Wee Reese, Gil Hodges, Roy Campanella, and most of all, Jackie Robinson. Dad turned us kids on to baseball and we all became rabid Mets fans; the hated Yankees, the Dodgers' bitter rival back in the 1950s, was not an option. My five brothers, my sister and I all played midget and high school sports as we grew up in our Long Island town, including baseball, softball, football, basketball and lacrosse, and a few of us played a college sport at a small time level. It was a lot of fun – certainly more fun than doing the homework we studiously tried to avoid.

With this background, I guess it was inevitable that I would turn my three kids, Joe, Ryan and Caroline on to sports. They have kept up the family tradition by becoming Mets fans and playing sports year round, and I've coached many of their teams as either head or assistant coach.

After my review of all these experiences, and a little independent study, it became clear to me that I had taken my kids' sports activities a little too seriously at times. On the positive side, this realization has helped me tremendously as I am now able to catch myself before I do anything stupid, like yell at a referee or opposing coach.

I also concluded that I know a helluva lot about this kids sports stuff. In fact, I'm an expert on the topic. I've seen it all, the good, the bad and ugly. And being the fair minded guy I am, I felt it would be very selfish of me to keep all of this keen insight to myself. So I figured I'd write this book to tell ya'll what I've learned about the wild world of youth sports.

In particular, take note of the parent characters that I identify in Chapter 1 including the Delusional Coach Dad, PC Team Mom, PC League President, Hypochondriac Mom, Evil Coach Dad and Hot Mom. If you are involved in youth sports, I guarantee that you will meet these people (if you haven't already). Perhaps you will even find that you are one of these parent types. On the other hand, if you determine that you do not fall into one of these categories, please don't hesitate to adopt my shameless stereotyping to ridicule your neighbors who do.

In addition, in the chapters that follow, I provide an insider's analysis of the kids sports culture that will give you parents out there a leg up on the parents who have failed to do their homework. Among other things, I give you the scoop on the dicey issues that sports parents inevitably face, including coach nepotism, travel team elitism, "other parent" conflicts, early specialization, politically correct cheering and the high school revisited culture that tends to emerge in the sports parent community. With this knowledge at your disposal, you'll have the answers to the difficult problems that tend to arise, such as:

- *What can you do about coaches favoring their own kid at your kid's expense?* Answer – Nothing man, your kid is screwed. All you can do is coach your own team. Then you will have the power to choose which innocent kids get the shaft so your kid can achieve the stardom he deserves.

- *How can you create and maintain good relationships with the parents of other kids on your child's team?* Answer Lighten their parental load by driving their kids to the team's games and practices and they'll love you.

- *What is the most common team stacking scam in youth sports?* Answer – The old "Assistant Coach Appointment Scheme," which I describe in detail in Chapter 4 along with other classic kids sports cons.

So I invite ya'll to read on for a more complete treatment of these and other kids sports questions that I've spent years studying. Please note that the personal anecdotes that I tell are true, but the names have been changed to protect the not so innocent. In addition, in a number of instances, characters I describe are a composite of folks I have met over the years, and are not patterned after any one person.

The book focuses on boys sports because most of my experiences have been in that arena. However, please be advised that my more limited observations of girls leagues have revealed that there are just as many dunderheads involved in them as in the boys leagues.

Finally, at the very end of our book, we introduce you to our new comic strip – *Joe Brady, Youth Sports Mogul*. We hope you enjoy it.

CHAPTER 1

THE CHARACTERS IN THE SHOW

The show that is the kids sports scene plays year around in virtually every U.S. town. It doesn't matter what part of the country the town is in, the same parent characters will be found coaching, driving kids to their games, and yelling on the sidelines. If you've been part of the scene, you'll recognize the parent types I identify in this chapter and know which of them should be avoided. If you are just getting started, take note so you can plot accordingly.

DELUSIONAL COACH DAD

Out he walks into the fresh spring air to the kingdom that he was meant to rule over. His confident and steady gait shows that he is a man in his element. He is the general who lives to lead his gallant shortstops and pitchers, but can never quite remember the name of his right fielder. His review of the scouting reports he keeps on his clipboard while he strides to the mound is clear evidence that he is smarter and better prepared than all those other coaches. More importantly, this ability to think and walk at the same time defies his wife's claim that he cannot multi-task.

As he aggressively directs his 8 year old players towards the goal of a little league championship, he'll maintain that it's not about him; no, no, it's about the kids. And in post-game meetings with parents, after screaming bloody murder for six innings, he'll quickly pivot to fallaciously present his altruistic side, and go on about how he loves to "teach" the kids and let them reap the benefits of his many years in the sports scene. In fact, only minutes into his post-game pontifications, he tends to not so subtly blurt out that he was quite a baseball player himself, and that he probably would have gone pro if it wasn't for the debilitating shoulder injury he suffered back in high school.

Yet despite all of his sports expertise, the kids he has coached have never quite developed the shortstop skills that his son has. Nor have any of his basketball players developed sufficient shooting skills to deprive his son of the twenty-five shots per game he deserves. Unfortunately, the coach thinks, these other kids just haven't measured up, and he must concede that even his expert coaching skills have their limits.

Who is this shallow man you ask? Answer – A "Delusional Coach Dad" (DCD). These are the dad coaches who get so caught up in their Tony LaRussa personas that they actually believe that they are real coaches. If you live in a typical American town, you most likely know a DCD. And ladies, you may, I'm sorry to say, even be married to one.

The first sign that a regular dad coach ("Coach Dad") is morphing into a DCD is a tendency to dress like a coach on a regular basis. If the dad you know constantly wears a whistle around his neck, regularly carries a clipboard, and has adopted an overall *White Shadow* kind of look, you most likely have a DCD on your hands. Other fashion indicators are more subtle, such as the excessive wearing of *Under Armour* jock wear and "Coach" jerseys.

An obvious DCD fashion indicator is the rare full uniform baseball coach look. Despite the admirable enthusiasm of the dudes who go with that getup, one can't help but wonder about them. I mean really, why would any 40 year old man go to the trouble of pulling a pair of skin-tight baseball pants over his fat ass every weekend morning so he can coach a bunch of 9 year olds? Answer – It's kinda like Halloween every Saturday and Sunday for him. He gets a break from wearing his Monday through Friday uniform (*i.e.*, a suit). Instead, the DCD gets to wear a baseball uniform while he instructs his little players, which gives him great pride and reinforces the delusion that he is a real coach.

Another strong DCD indicator is a coach's decision to wear cleats while he leads his team of children. Upon reflection, I think you will agree that there is no practical reason for a dad to make the cleats move. Kids coaches do not need extra traction while they pace the sidelines, keep the score book or wave runners around third base. In fact, coaches can do these jobs just as effectively, and far more comfortably, in a soft pair of sneakers.

So then why do dads go with the cleats look? Answer – Whether consciously or subconsciously these dads are sending a message consistent with their DCD self-image – that they should be taken seriously. By donning the cleats, the DCD puts the parents and other coaches on notice that he is not one of those amateurish fathers who merely wear sneakers while leading their teams. Hell no, the cleats certify that he is the genuine article.

The typical DCD also brings a "win at all costs" mentality to his team of children. This mentality can manifest itself in many ways, most notably draft rigging, yelling at umpires, running up scores, repeated references to Bobby Knight in pep talks, and the rejection of minimum play requirements (which are rules that require all the players on a team to play a significant part of each game).

Conversely, DCDs tend to be sore losers. This behavior mimics the boorish, never take responsibility style that we've all seen over the years at post-game press conferences from famous coaches like Knight and Bill Parcells. These star coaches are constantly talking about how their players must "step up," but when their teams lose they blame everybody but themselves. Consistent with this "point the finger" approach, the typical DCD will concoct excuses for the losses he suffers, such as a lack of talent on his team, a bad umpire, the failure of a key player to make the game, or a "sleepover" that robbed the kids of their intensity.

But what, you may ask, has caused the many DCDs throughout the U.S. to become so obsessed and oblivious to reality?

Well, I've found that certain personality types tend to evolve into DCDs. The first is the ultra-competitive Type A dad. In this category, you'll find successful corporate managers, entrepreneurs, and occasionally dads who actually played sports at a high level. These are the "driven" guys who must win at all costs, even if it's just a soccer match between 6 year olds. To these dudes, youth sports ain't no fun and games – it's serious business. And this serious approach often pays off for the Type As as they tend to win league championships, just as they've successfully climbed the corporate ladder or created their own thriving businesses.

The second common DCD personality type is the much referred to "frustrated jock," who is driven by a feeling of inadequacy left over from his own, dreadful childhood sports experiences. These feelings cause the frustrated jock to compensate for his childhood nightmares by seeking success through his kid's teams. Professor Frank L. Smoll, a University of Washington psychologist who has written many books on youth sports, says that these frustrated jock dads take on a sense of "over-identification" by "becom[ing] dependent on the youngster for feelings of self worth."

This phenomenon, of the adult male trying to overcome his childhood sports failures, is firmly embedded in American pop culture through movies that most of us sports fans have seen. For example, in *The Best of Times*, Robin Williams plays a banker who never got over dropping a touchdown pass in a high school football game. In *The Benchwarmers*, Jon Lovetts plays a dweeb turned billionaire who puts together a team of nerds that beats the hell out of a bunch of jock filled squads on their way to the championship game. In *The Mighty Ducks*, Emilio Estevez plays a lawyer whose promising hockey career was cut short by injury before he could make it to the NHL. However, dissatisfied with his law practice, the Estevez character gives it up and returns to the sport he loves to coach a bunch of rag-a-muffin kids to victory over the evil Russians.

All these stories are based on a redemption theme wherein the hero strives to overcome his childhood demons and achieve sports success. This is exactly what many DCDs are seeking by winning a T-Ball championship or two – redemption, a day in the sun after all those years of failure.

Of course, even the most emotionally balanced Coach Dads can, on occasion, forget that crushing the other team of children is bad form. For example, one time I pulled a Barry Switzer on an unsuspecting soccer coach. I'm sure ya'll remember how Barry Switzer, the former University of Oklahoma football coach, used to run up the score against some of the chump teams his squad played. During the 1986 and 1987 seasons for instance, Oklahoma won by scores of 63-0, 64-3, 77-0, 69-14, 65-0, 56-3, 59-10 and 71-10.

Well, one Saturday morning in 2006 I would have made Barry proud. At the time, I was an assistant coach of Ryan's soccer team, which played in a league for kids about 6 years old. We were winning like 15 to 0, and during the game, Ryan had perfected a Terrell Owens-like hot dog goal scoring celebration. After each goal that he scored, Ryan would pull his jersey over the top of his head and scream like a crazed college drunk during spring break as he sprinted back to the middle of the field. In contrast, the players on the other team could barely figure out which direction to kick the ball, and it seemed like two or three of them were crying the entire game.

Near the end of the match, the opposing coach broke the rules when he had one of his kids play goalie even though it was a no goalie league. You'd think that I would have had a little sympathy for the guy being that we were killing his team of little children and the match was almost over. But *nooooooo*, slaughtering the other team wasn't enough. It only whet my appetite for an even bigger win. So, after the goalie stopped a couple of shots, I aggressively told the coach that he was violating the rules by placing a goalie on the field. As I said this, the guy sent me an intense "I'll kill you" kind of glare. Luckily, the match ended a few minutes later and I got out of there quickly, before he could kick my ass.

When I reflected on my Barry Switzer moment afterwards, I felt horrible. How could I have been so shallow and so absurdly combative while leading my little soccer players? Looking to make some sense of my behavior, I discussed the event with Joe, who was 10 at the time. Joe confirmed the obvious, I was a loser.

And that's really the point for all of us parents who are able to view the kids sports scene from a moderately balanced perspective – don't turn into a win-at-all-costs loser while coaching youth sports. Leave the loser type behavior to the true DCDs in your town. That way you can mock them at neighborhood barbecues and cocktail parties with a clear conscience.

DELUSIONAL COACH DAD

AT A GLANCE

CHILDHOOD SPORTS HIGHLIGHT:	THE TIME HE WASN'T PICKED LAST
FAVORITE DESIGNER:	UNDER ARMOUR
PRIMARY COACHING TECHNIQUE:	SCREAM THE DESIRED RESULT (I.E., "THROW STRIKES!", "TACKLE HIM!")
SIGNATURE MOVE:	ASSISTANT COACH DRAFT SCHEME

KNOW-IT-ALL DAD

These dads are the self-proclaimed sports experts who ramble on endlessly in the stands about the ongoing game and the tactics the coaches should employ. Although these guys are often loud, they rarely add anything of substance. Much like the DCD, the typical Know-It-All Dad will do nothing more than shout out result based clichés such as "hit the ball" or "play defense." These dudes have no idea how the kids can be taught to do these things, they just want them done.

Even worse than the generic result demanders are the Know-It-All Dads who insert themselves into the game by yelling out strategies to the kids, such as "take the first pitch," "look for the fast break" or "pressure the ball." Of course, the instructions from these back seat drivers are often different from those given by the real coach, which confuses the hell out of the kids and wrecks the coach's game plan. But such things do not deter these local Tim McCarvers from being heard. Besides, they're covered regardless of the outcome. If the team wins, the back seat driver will claim that his instructions propelled the kids to victory. On the other hand, if the team loses, it's always the real coach's fault.

The boaster is yet another species within the Know-It-All Dad category. These self-involved types will go on and on about such things as his kid's latest homer, touchdown or hat trick. And, of course, boasters never miss an opportunity to announce their high status in the kids sports community by repeated references to the various "travel" and "all-star" teams their kid plays on. Lastly, no extended conversation with a true boaster will pass without a reference to the college scholarship his kid will undoubtedly earn. Needless to say, conversations with these guys must be avoided at all costs.

Finally, the worst of the Know-It-All Dad lot are the ones who step over the line from obnoxious to juvenile by screaming at referees when they allegedly blow a call. I've never been able to figure these angry men out. And, at this point, I've given up analyzing their extreme form of frustrated jockness. All I know is what my parents told me many years ago – if the crowd you hang with are all potheads, you probably are too. And so it goes with the Know-It-All Dad referee abusers. If you've been standing next to one of these dudes in the stands all season, other parents will assume that you're also a whacko. In such cases, you must take action to save your reputation. Whether it be moving to the other team's stands, or blowing the games off altogether, just get your butt away from the mad man before you become guilty by association.

The Know-It-All Dad dresses in a variety of styles. Some play the part of the former jock by wearing sweat outfits while they talk the talk. Others, usually residing in upper middle class suburbs, appear in GQ type weekend outfits, such as polo shirts and cardigan sweaters. And others go with the jeans, t-shirt and sneakers look.

Whatever the fashion style, the classic Know-It-All Dad tends to plant himself in conspicuous spots, like in the middle of the stands or a prime sideline location, so he can be seen as well as heard. Some teams get stuck with a whole group of Know-It-All Dads who sit together during the games. Like any faction, leaders and followers emerge within these groups. If the leader is a yeller, other dads yell. If the leader provides a PC type of vibe, the other dads whisper their criticisms throughout the game. Whatever the vibe, what inevitably develops is a forum for the dads to impress each other with their commentary on their kids' team and the sports issues of the day.

Me, a Know-It-All Dad? Has my sideline behavior earned me a membership in the Know-It-All Dad club you ask? No way, I'm not one of those losers. I'm well informed, mature and fair. When I choose to speak at a ballgame, I do not speak solely for the benefit of my kids. I have a much higher goal when I address the public. In fact, each and every one of my Saturday morning bleacher comments is intended to improve our community and our society as a whole.

Yeah, I know, you're not buying this. The truth is that I consider myself a low level Know-It-All Dad. I'm not a yeller and do not regularly sit with any group of dads. I prefer to privately revel in my kids' successes and think bad thoughts about the coach and the other little players when my kids are going bad.

But there have been a few periods during which I just had to reveal my true genius to all who would listen. As I boldly spoke my mind during those several basketball seasons, I was like Dean Smith, Adolph Rupp and John Wooden wrapped into one person. I educated the crowd on the fundamentals and provided insightful commentary on the games taking place before us. After all, in 1979 I played on a high school basketball team and went out with a cheerleader. With these credentials in hand, it was clear to me during those seasons in which I spoke so eloquently that I was providing a great service to those parents who weren't blessed with my sports pedigree. Of course, my high school hoops team sucked and the cheerleader dumped me. But hey, the parents I so cleverly impressed will never know that will they.

KNOW-IT-ALL DAD

AT A GLANCE	
TV IDOL:	BILL SWERSKI
SOURCE OF ALL EXPERTISE:	SPORTS CENTER
PRIMARY PERSONALITY TRAIT:	IRREPRESSIBLE WILL TO BE HEARD
SIGNATURE MOVE:	POST-GAME I TOLD YOU SO

TEAM MOM/TEAM MANAGER

The Team Mom or Team Manager is a mom who organizes team activities by, among other things, notifying the parents of the times and locations of practices and games, arranging carpools, providing directions to field locations, collecting money for fund raisers, and assigning team snack duties. This would seem to be a somewhat innocuous job that would not result in much variation among the women who take it on. However, there are two types of Team Moms that tend to emerge.

The "June Cleaver Team Mom" maintains a sunny disposition, genuinely tries to help the coaches do their job, and makes life easier for other parents as they attempt to meet all of their responsibilities. They are a pleasure to work with because they do their job without conflict and judgment, and they have no agenda other than helping the best way they can.

In contrast, the "PC Team Moms" are horrible. These are the moms who are there – in their own mind – to keep everything under control, apply the latest PC doctrine to the job, and gossip about those parents who fail to conform to the rules. You know you are stuck with one of these types when you are bombarded with e-mails enforcing team snack, parent cheering and mandatory cup wearing rules. And how these ladies delight in disapproving of slackers who fail to get their kids to practice on time or forget to submit the raffle ticket money they were assigned to collect. Such parents are labeled as deviants by the PC Team Mom, and they are punished via her cold shoulder for the rest of the season.

Some PC Team Moms seem to reserve a particular animus for the working moms of kids on the team, many of whom can't devote much time to team activities. Far be it from me to figure out what's going on in *any* woman's mind, but such targeted spite must reflect some kind of insecurity, jealousy or inner dissatisfaction. Whatever the reason, I have no doubt that Helen Reddy would be really pissed off if she ever found out about this abuse of working women.

PC TEAM MOM

AT A GLANCE

ANALOGOUS MOVIE CHARACTER:	BABS JANSEN
FAVORITE PAST TIME:	EXCLUDING PEOPLE
HER VITALLY IMPORTANT CAUSE:	HEALTHY SNACK ENFORCEMENT
SIGNATURE MOVE:	DISMISSIVE HEAD TURN

LEAGUE PRESIDENT

Kids league presidents can have a tremendous impact on the lives of parents by the rules they make and by their overall competency or lack thereof. There are several types of managerial styles that these guys and gals utilize that, for better or worse, mirror the styles of famous politicians that we all know.

<u>Harding President</u>. Our 29th president, Warren G. Harding, led an administration that is regarded as one of the most corrupt in U.S. history. Historians have written that Harding was not personally corrupt. Rather, he was a figure head type president who let his crooked cronies run amok causing scandal after scandal, the most prominent of which was the Teapot Dome controversy.

It is this very same type of lax oversight by kids league presidents that leads to corruption. In such instances, the policies that leagues have in place to protect the weak, such as minimum play requirements, are disregarded, and drafts are rigged by win-at-all cost DCDs so they get the best players every year. Believe me, I've attended many of these drafts, and when they are not administered by a strong league officer, shark DCDs use every trick in the book to gain an advantage.

Simply put, the Harding President is too weak to be an effective leader. While I would never want any kids league president's term to end like President Harding's did in 1923 – by heart attack and death – parents should look to replace any Harding type presidents that they are stuck with as soon as possible.

<u>Lincoln President</u>. Sure, giving any kids league officer the "Lincoln" label trivializes the great accomplishments of our 16th president. It goes without saying that a league president's

organization of a successful bake sale could never match Lincoln's perseverant leadership of the North to victory during our painful Civil War. But, then again, Lincoln never had to face the wrath of an enraged soccer mom upset over her little boy's lack of playing time.

Most of us would agree that Lincoln provided a great pearl of wisdom when he said, "Always bear in mind that your own resolution to succeed is more important than any other one thing." But, if Lincoln was a kids league president today, such an emphasis on winning would be seen by the PC crowd as an overly aggressive, male domineering type of attitude that viciously subjects kids to hurt feelings (when they lose). Faced with the unrelenting ire of the child psychologists who reside in his town, and groups of Oprahfied moms, Lincoln would be forced to capitulate to their demand for a "don't keep score" rule that would save the children from such emotional scarring.

As these hypothetical challenges to Lincoln's genius show, the most difficult task for any league president in today's kids sports market is the implementation of rules that balance things out for the lesser talented kids, while still allowing the athletic kids a forum to compete. Presidents can only do this if they are confident, decisive and have the political savvy to keep all the factions (*i.e.*, PC police, aggressive DCDs, etc.) happy. The few presidents who are able to walk this fine line are worthy of the "Lincoln" label.

Marcos President. The Marcos president, named after the late despotic president of the Philippines, Ferdinand Marcos, is an utterly corrupt person who uses his office to enrich himself at the expense of the league, the parents and the kids. I have never personally run into such a scoundrel, but there are many out there.

For example, in 2008, Jim Nehmans, the former Mayor of Adelanto California and one time president of the Adelanto Little League, was found guilty for stealing more than $20,000 from the league. And, in 2007, Paul Roth, Jr., a former president and treasurer of the Vista California Little league, was sentenced to six months in jail for stealing more than $21,000 from the Vista league.

So parents, while most league officials are good natured people, you still have to keep an eye on them – they are politicians after all.

<u>PC President</u>. PC Presidents are primarily concerned with implementing the latest politically correct policies. They have little interest in developing athletes or, God forbid, teaching kids how to win games. Instead, these presidents obsessively focus on such things as parent codes of conduct, maintaining no keeping score rules, and mandatory trophy presentations. While these league officers appear to be well intentioned, they seem oblivious to the natural instinct of most boys – they want to win the game.

The worst of this lot see themselves as a force of good who have taken on the task of teaching the unenlightened masses (*i.e.*, the rest of us) how to behave. This education is not limited to sports-related issues. No, these all-knowing do-gooders take on the task of teaching us how to live our lives. Thus, they will lecture us through league regulations and policies about the foods we should feed our children, and deprive us of our first amendment rights by dictating the content of our cheering.

Some of these low-level bureaucrats will even use their kids sports position as a forum to lecture the rest of us on the "enlightened" parenting philosophies that we all should adhere to. Hell, as of summer 2012, one soccer league in my state provided the parents with a "Ten Commandments for Soccer Parents," the first of which declares that parents "shall not impose your ambitions on your child." The third commandment, I kid you not, includes a footnote notifying parents of the obvious, that "Your job is to...love your child."

So what's the bottom line with respect to the PC Presidents out there? You just have to watch them. I believe in many of the things they tend to implement, such as minimum play requirements. However, any kids league president who lectures parents as to how they should raise their children is way out of bounds.

PC PRESIDENT

AT A GLANCE	
PURPOSE IN LIFE:	TO FIX PEOPLE
PRIMARY PERSONALITY TRAIT:	GOD COMPLEX
SENSE OF HUMOR?	NO
SIGNATURE MOVE:	CONDESCENDING TONE

HOT MOM

Unfortunately, kids sports leagues are dominated by a group of pretty ugly guys – us Coach Dads. We're generally loud, self-important, fashion-challenged blowhards, who blather on endlessly about sports issues we know very little about. Luckily, there are always a large contingent of moms at ballgames to brighten the scenery.

Of course, in today's superficial culture, the most attractive women within a community tend to achieve more notoriety than the others, and the youth sports community is no exception. Which leads me to the "Hot Mom". What's a Hot Mom you ask? Well, it should be self-explanatory to you dudes out there. But essentially, these women are, in a word, hot. It's not the classic Miss America type of beauty, which would be an unfair measure for any 40 year old mom. Instead, think Teri Hatcher and Nicole Sheridan, it's more of a gum snappin' Desperate Housewifeish type of look.

As one might expect, Hot Moms are usually married to rich dudes. Regular middle class guys just can't afford the designer clothes, spas, personal trainers and vacation homes that many Hot Moms require. Unlike the "Team Mom," the Hot Mom is not interested in helping with team or league activities. Rather, the Hot Mom is intensely focused on staying thin and maintaining her good looks.

While this lack of participation is somewhat troubling, is it really fair to criticize the Hot Moms for their lack of involvement? In my view, it's really a matter of intent, as it is with any alleged crime. Thus, within the Hot Mom category, there are both *good* Hot Moms, who have no bad intentions, and *bad* Hot Moms, who do.

With respect to the good Hot Mom, think Chrissie Snow (*i.e.,* Suzanne Somers) from *Three's Company.* You know that after she moved out of her apartment with Jack and Janet she met some rich guy, got married and had kids. If you ever observed Chrissie's dim persona at any length, you gotta know that she couldn't have provided much help organizing the kids leagues in her town. But can you really blame a Chrissie Snow type for being too confused to meet both her workout schedule and the kids' practice schedule? Really, she means no harm.

With respect to the bad Hot Mom, think Amanda Woodward (*i.e.,* Heather Locklear) from *Melrose Place.* If Amanda ever moved out of LA to some suburb and had kids, she'd have the other moms driving them to games all over town so she could spend more time at the office screwing people over. And she'd seduce dazed Coach Dads into giving her kids the starting shortstop and quarterback positions. In contrast to the Chrissie Snow type, the Amanda Woodward Hot Mom is a bad, bad woman who cannot be trusted.

All in all, you have to give the Hot Moms their due. Sure, they're easy targets because they're self-centered and shallow. But can we really expect them to help out at a ballgame, when it takes so much work to keep up those looks? While many of us have achieved very little in life, the typical Hot Mom has achieved something – hotness. This may have been easy for them at the age of seventeen, but it takes a tremendous amount of dedication and work to maintain such high standards at the age of 40.

In keeping up their fantastic appearance year after year, the Hot Moms have all the characteristics of our greatest American heroes. They demonstrate an irrepressible work ethic by never missing a day at the gym, unmatched perseverance by becoming even more blonde year after year, and great ingenuity by taking advantage of the latest technologies, whether it be liposuction, breast enhancements or miracle creams. Indeed, these women are far more successful at achieving the tangible "stay hot" goal they've set for themselves than most of us have been at achieving our "career" goals. For this, I salute you Hot Moms, and thank you for showing us all that living out the Great American Dream is still possible.

HOT MOM

AT A GLANCE	
FAVORITE BOOK:	**PEOPLE MAGAZINE'S FIFTY MOST BEAUTIFUL PEOPLE**
FAVORITE HOBBY:	**INVESTMENT BANKERS**
HER GUIDING RULE IN LIFE:	**JENNIFER – GOOD, ANGELINA – BAD**
SIGNATURE MOVE:	**LOW-CUT TANK TOP**

EVIL COACH DAD

While the typical DCD will occasionally make an ass of himself and thereby embarrass the hell out of his family, most of them aren't bad guys deep down inside. They're just shooting for a little glory through their kids' sports experience. However, there's a whole other rare category of Coach Dads who are very dangerous – the *Evil* Coach Dad.

We all knew a couple of these bad eggs as kids. They were the ones who pushed little children into pools, threw ice balls at kids' faces, and tortured small animals. When they got to high school they groped girls in the halls, cheated on tests, and beat up nerds. Well guess what? These guys grew up and *some of them coach kids sports*!

I know, some of you are probably saying, c'mon how evil could a coach of little children really be? Well, the answer is Satan like, just read the papers. For example, there's Mark Downs, a Pennsylvania T-Ball coach. According to media reports, in 2005, Downs offered Keith Reese Jr., one of his 8 year old players, $25 to throw a baseball at Harry Bowers, an autistic teammate, before a playoff game. Downs' plan was to injure Bowers and knock him out of the game to increase the team's chances of winning.

The first ball that Reese threw hit Bowers in the groin. However this didn't satisfy Downs, who then instructed Reese to hit Bowers harder. Following orders, Reese threw the ball at Bowers and hit him in the ear. After his plan was uncovered, Downs was convicted of corruption of minors and conspiracy to commit simple assault and sentenced to one to six years in jail. How's that for evil?

Then there's the story of Shaun Farr and Bob Farley, coaches of the Yankees, a 10 and under team in the Bountiful, Utah little league. In a June 2006 championship game, the Yankees were up by one run over the Red Sox in the bottom of the last inning with two outs and a man on third. When Farr and Farley realized that the Red Sox' best hitter, Jordan Bleak, was coming to bat, they ordered the Yankees' pitcher to walk Bleak intentionally, and the pitcher carried out the order.

While the decision to walk the 10 year old Bleak was questionable in its own right, the story gets worse. The batter who followed Bleak, the kid who Farr and Farley put in the unenviable position of batting with the Red Sox' whole season on the line, was Romney Oaks, an undersized 9 year old brain cancer survivor. Romney's ability to play baseball had been severely damaged by years of chemotherapy and other treatments. But he continued to play just so he could feel like a regular kid. *The Salt Lake Tribune* reported that Romney wore a helmet while he played the outfield "to guard the shunt in his head [and] [w]hen he swung the bat, it looked like a drag bunt."

So when Farr and Farley put Romney on the spot, in a no win situation, it was no surprise that Romney struck out as the tears rolled down his face. Farr rationalized his ruthless tactic by contending that winning the game somehow justified crushing the spirit of a physically debilitated boy when he said: "It wasn't about picking on a cancer survivor. It was about taking the bat out of their best hitter's hands in order to win." But in a game between 9 and 10 year olds? Sorry Coach Farr, it just doesn't compute.

So how do you know if there's an Evil Coach Dad coaching kids in your town? Well, many of them can be tough to spot at first glance because they've learned to camouflage their evil ways by such things as leading community organizations and wearing authentic polo shirts. Nevertheless, there are a number of signs that I recommend parents watch for to expose Evil Coach Dads in their midst:

- He has a win at all costs mentality – even for 5 and 6 year olds.

- He has no empathy for the less athletic kids and belittles them when they make bad plays.

- He constantly yells at his players.

- He and his team refuse to shake hands after games.

- He has a mustache, a fashion preference traditionally selected by villains that connotes an overall sneaky disposition a la Snidely Whiplash.

- He runs up the score when his team is winning.

- He trash talks kids on opposing teams.

- He drives a Porsche or some other trophy sports car indicating a troubling superficiality that corresponds to his childish need to be recognized as the winner of the first place trophy in a league for small children.

- He teaches his kids to play dirty by such methods as throwing elbows in basketball or brush back pitches in baseball.

- He's a lawyer.

Perhaps the most reliable Evil Coach Dad indicator is the tendency to wear black while coaching. Just think about it people, who wears black on a regular basis? Are you drawing a blank? Let me help you out. Ya got Hells Angels, the Oakland Raiders, Dracula, and yes, Evil Coach Dads. For example, what did Wolf Stansson wear when he was torturing Emilio Estevez and the Mighty Ducks? Answer – black sweat suits and business suits. What about Roy Turner, the evil coach of the Yankees in the *Bad News Bears*? Answer – he liked the black team jacket look. And what about Coach Jay Hoffer, the evil coach in *The Big Green*? Answer – black sweat pants, black shirts, black team jacket, black cap. Need I go on?

So parents, if your kid's coach demonstrates a preference for black clothes, beware, you may have a big problem on your hands.

EVIL COACH DAD

AT A GLANCE	
IDOL:	WOLF STANSSON
HIS COMPETITIVE ADVANTAGE:	THE IRRELEVANCE OF PROVINCIAL MIDDLE CLASS VALUES
FAVORITE AUTHOR:	CHARLES DARWIN
SIGNATURE MOVE:	THE BREAKING OF A CHILD'S SPIRIT

COOL COACH

Most of us kids coaches can be described as anything but "cool."

We don't look cool wearing pieced together "coach" outfits comprised of such things as ill-fitting sweat pants, ugly team jerseys, and high top sneakers.

Our behavior is the opposite of cool. We intensely pace the sidelines as if the result of the game before us will resolve the global economic crisis. We whine like spoiled brats when the referee or umpire makes a bad call, and we excitedly yell instructions that the kids often ignore.

However, most towns have one or two "Cool Coaches," who make the rest of us coaches look bad. These are the type of guys who have been cool all of their lives. They were the Zack Morris of their high school and the Eric Stratton of their college. They do not dress up like a "real" coach in the way the DCDs do. Instead, they go with an understated weekend coach kind of look that conveys the message that they know that kids sports is not serious business. Naturally, they have good hair that looks oh so cool under their baseball caps. Bald guys like me are *ipso facto* uncool, and are thus barred from the "Cool Coach" club for life.

The Cool Coach is calm and apparently oblivious to the pressure of the game, says the right things to all the parents, and gives the appearance of not caring whether the team wins or loses. Hell, why would he care if he loses a game or two, he's won in life. After a loss by his team of children, he still gets to hop in his luxury car with his hot wife and drive to his big house. Of course, the fact that he's got a hot wife does not stop him from getting a little action on the side when the situation presents itself.

Despite his nonchalance, the Cool Coach will win more often than not. Picture Colonel Hogan from *Hogan's Heroes* manipulating his German captors to achieve victory under their noses. Only in the kids sports scenario, the rest of us coaches are Schultz and Colonel Klink, and Hogan, the Cool Coach, outwits us every time.

COOL COACH

AT A GLANCE	
OCCUPATION:	RETIRED
SECRET TO SUCCESS:	THREE WORDS – CONFIDENCE, CONFIDENCE, CONFIDENCE
GREATEST GIFT BESIDES STUDLY FEATURES:	ABILITY TO FEIGN EMPATHY
SIGNATURE MOVE:	NEGLECTED HOT MOM SWOOP

"I DON'T GIVE A CRAP" PARENT

There is no question that parents today are more involved in their kids' sports endeavors than parents of prior generations. We spend a fortune on new gear, personal coaches and sports camps. We drive hundreds of miles on weekends to get our kids to their travel team games. We obsess about whether our kids are getting a fair shake from their coaches. But, more than anything else, we attend the games to cheer our kids on.

Back in the day, many parents could not make their kids' ballgames because they had real life responsibilities to attend to, such as working a second job or taking care of house work. In fact, some parents would rarely make a game. However, nobody gave it a second thought because kids just fended for themselves in those days.

Things are far different in the era of the "helicopter" parent. "Thou shalt attend all thy kids' games" has become a commandment of the sports parent religion, and parents who regularly miss games are conspicuously absent.

But is it fair to label parents as "bad" for missing a few T-Ball games in a given season? The answer is no. Having gone through periods when work has prevented me from attending my kids' games, I fully understand why many parents can't make *all* the games. However, there are certain parents who so completely disregard the quality of their kids' sports experience that they rightly earn the "I Don't Give a Crap Parent" label. The following are several of the ways parents can attain this dreaded designation (either by itself or in combination depending on the degree of abuse):

39

1. *The failure to attend at least some of the kid's games in a given season.* The message from the parent to the child by this behavior is unmistakable – the parent just doesn't care.

2. *The failure to dress the kid appropriately and provide the basic equipment.* For example, any kid who shows up to the first practice of a new baseball season with a plastic glove wearing hush puppies is screwed. The ball will bounce out of the glove all practice, and the other kids will label him as a nerd for his lame footwear, all of which will put the kid at the bottom of the coach's depth chart and the bottom of the kids' cool chart.

3. *Excessive smoking of crack on the sidelines.* (Sorry I couldn't pass that up. Please move on to No. 4.)

4. *The failure to prepare a kid for organized sports.* Yes, the Type A DCDs who begin training their kids for athletic stardom at the age of 2 are way over the top. But the I Don't Give a Crap Parent who never bothers to play catch with his son before he signs him up for baseball for the first time at the age of 10 is just cruel. By that age, most of the other boys will have played organized baseball for several years. Consequently, the I Don't Give a Crap Parent's kid will have no chance whatsoever of succeeding in his new baseball venture. Even worse, when it becomes obvious that the kid sucks, he will be the subject of ridicule from his teammates and derisive whispers from parents. No parent should put his kid through this type of hell.

5. *The failure to get the child to practice and games on time or at all.* This puts the kid in the coach's dog house resulting in reduced playing time, which reduces the kid's chance to improve.

I DON'T GIVE A CRAP PARENT

AT A GLANCE

MOTTO:	**DO NOT TODAY WHAT CAN BE LEFT UNTIL TOMORROW**
ALL TOO CONVENIENT PARENTING PHILOSOPHY:	**HELICOPTER PARENTING DETERS CHILD INDEPENDENCE**
FAVORITE BALLPARK SPOT:	**THE CONCESSION STAND**
SIGNATURE MOVE:	**"I'LL MAKE THE NEXT GAME SON"**

HYPOCHONDRIAC MOM

Among the moms attending most any ballgame, a "Hypochondriac Mom" can be found. She's the one with the worried look on her face slapping the sunscreen on her kid between innings; rushing water bottles over to the kid after a harrowing (in her mind) run from third to home; or insisting that the child wear a fluffy winter jacket under his soccer jersey on a brisk October morning.

When they're not dashing into the dugout to save their child from the latest potential disaster, the Hypochondriac Moms hover in and around the stands looking for an opportunity to scare the hell out of other moms with stories about such things as the dangers of aluminum bats and peanut butter. So, unless you're up for a good dose of pessimism, conversations with these ladies are not recommended.

HYPOCHONDRIAC MOM

AT A GLANCE

FAVORITE SIDELINE TOPICS:	VACCINATIONS, PEANUT BUTTER
MOST ABUSIVE HM MOVE:	WINTER JACKET UNDER TEAM JERSEY MANDATE
ACCESSORIES:	WATER BOTTLE, SUN BLOCK, HEALTHY SNACKS
SIGNATURE MOVE:	NEGATIVE CONVERSATION TURN

THE "IMPORTANT" BUSINESSMAN

This is a very important man, the Important Businessman. On weekends, he comes to the field prepared with his chair – not to watch his little Brandon play little league, but to read the latest business news or catch up on critical "office" work. If possible, after he parks his Range Rover, he'll take a inconspicuous route onto the ball field and set up his things in an isolated area of the field, away from the parents, where he can sit and read his *Wall Street Journal*, *Financial Times* or company reports.

If no back door path is available, he'll take the pain, the pain of exchanging meaningless small talk with parents as he makes his way to his coveted lawn chair haven, far, far away from people who actually care about the game and the trite town tales that they exchange. I mean really, how could anyone expect a businessman, such as the Important Businessman, to give a crap about Bill Salmon's new lawn mower when so many important business decisions are yet to be made?

When he finally achieves his isolated spot, the Important Businessman plunges into his reading, gathering information that will propel him to success the following week. He will not be interrupted, except, of course, by urgent cell phone calls and emails from office colleagues and potential deal partners.

Despite his continuous focus on his work, the Important Businessman is not oblivious to the fact that he is a dad who must meet the obligations he has to his child. To achieve this goal, the Important Businessman occasionally looks up from his work to see if Brandon has taken his turn at bat. Fortunately, the Important Businessman need not do so until the third inning because little Brandon bats dead last in the order, and plays right field where balls are rarely hit. Every half an hour or so, the Important Businessman keeps up Brandon's spirits by waving to him as he looks to his dad for approval. When Brandon runs out to his dad's spot along the left field line between innings, to ask the Important Businessman if he saw his hit, a dribbler along the first base line, the Important Businessman has the good sense to lie and claim that he did.

During the work week, the Important Businessman is, unfairly, faced with a dilemma that businessmen of prior generations never had to deal with. Back in the day, it was socially acceptable for dads to miss their kids' sporting events while they brought home the bacon. But these days absentee fathering is no longer socially acceptable, and even dads such as the Important Businessman must show up at their kids' games to avoid hurting their feelings. Consequently, the Important Businessman's wife is constantly complaining that he is the only dad in the entire town who never makes his boy's weeknight games.

So to keep his woman quiet, the Important Businessman makes the effort to catch the end of a weeknight game or two. On those rare occasions, the Important Businessman arrives at the field in the fifth or sixth inning sporting a suit or a blazer. In between emails and phone calls, the Important Businessman impatiently puts in his time watching the little boys flub grounders, and engages in small talk with annoying, less important, parents. As the final out is made, the Important Businessman quickly calls Brandon over and ushers him into the Range Rover. On the way home, the Important Businessman dutifully continues the lie, "yes Brandon, I saw your bunt hit in the third inning."

Upon arriving home, the Important Businessman congratulates himself. The trip to Brandon's game was a success. Yes, he lost about an hour's work time. But, on the positive side, the fifth inning appearance will minimize his wife's complaints for a day or two – and there is certainly value in that.

IMPORTANT BUSINESSMAN

AT A GLANCE	
CHILDHOOD HERO:	JACK WELCH
PRIMARY PERSONALITY TRAIT:	ARROGANCE
FAVORITE TV SHOW:	JOURNAL EDITORIAL REPORT
SIGNATURE MOVE:	"EXCUSE ME I HAVE TO TAKE THIS CALL"

CHEERING MOMS

Not to get overly serious on ya'll, but when this sports stuff is said and done, when my time watching my kids play ball is over, I will miss many things. Most of all, I will miss being with Joe, Ryan and Caroline while we lived our sports life together. In fact, the mere thought of those times with them passing me by makes me sick, very sick.

Other, less personal, aspects of the kids sports culture will also be sorely missed, including the joy of little boys and girls as they arrive at first base; seeing a kid gain confidence as a season progresses; pleasant chats with friends in the bleachers; and kids cheering on their teammates through a chain link backstop.

Out of the many sounds one hears at a kids game, the one that I will probably miss the most is the sound of moms cheering on their children. When I think of times gone by, this sound comes to me as I see myself walking from my car to the baseball field on a warm spring Saturday. First, I hear the ping of the bat, and then the loud Cheering Mom shrieks: "run baby run;" "go, go, go;" "slide, slide!" My interest piqued by the excited moms, I jog to the field hoping that my kid was part of the big play.

At the down points of games, when their kids strike out, drop pop-ups or blow layups, the Cheering Moms are quick to shout words of encouragement: "good try Sammy, good try;" "don't worry Oliver you'll get 'em next time;" "great swing, great swing."

Whether it be the bottom of the sixth and two runs down, four touchdowns back in the fourth quarter, or five goals behind in the second half, the Cheering Moms never say die. Instead, they preach perseverance and accentuate the positive: "C'mon Tigers, you got 'em;" "Go Ridgefield;" "Nice shot Patrick;" "Great pitch Jason."

Yes, the sound of Cheering Moms at a kids ball game is a sweet, sweet sound. I thank God I will get to hear it many more times before I am forced to move on.

CHEERING MOMS

AT A GLANCE	
NO. 1 POWER:	PURE LOVE
SIGNATURE MOVE:	NEVER SAY DIE CHEER
DISPOSITION:	SUNNY, RESILIENT
EVER PRESENT DANGER:	VICARIOUS FAILURE PAIN

CHAPTER 2

HOW COME OUR FIRST BASEMAN CAN'T CATCH?

After years of jealously watching kids ride up and down the block in their baseball uniforms, Jim convinces his 9 year old son, Billy, to give little league a try. As a lifelong fan of the Great American Pastime, Jim is excited about watching Billy play the game in its purest form. Yes, Jim's time has arrived. Finally, little Billy will begin his march toward the glory that should have been Jim's. The glory that was stolen from Jim by numerous, know nothing, little league coaches who failed to recognize his skills and overall flair for the game.

To prepare Billy, Jim plays catch with him in the cold wet March evenings. Soon Billy gets a phone call from his coach, and the joy that is little league begins. Billy's practices are held in the afternoons while Jim is at work, and after the third practice, Billy tells Jim that he has been playing outfield. Of course, Jim is aware that outfield isn't the most glamorous position to play at the age of 9. But Jim is not disturbed by the coach's initial failure to recognize Billy's talent because the league has a rule that requires coaches to play all the kids at infield positions during the season. This rule gives Jim great comfort because it mandates that Billy will get a fair shake.

On opening day, Billy's team runs onto the field for the first inning, except for one fat kid, who plods out of the dugout far behind the others. Jim's eyes follow the fat kid's painfully slow movements as he finally stops at first base and starts throwing ground balls to the other infielders. As Jim watches Billy warm-up in right field, he jokingly thinks to himself that the first baseman must be the next Boog Powell.

Soon enough, the game begins. The first batter hits a ground ball to the second baseman, who catches it and makes the easy toss to little Boog. As the ball approaches little Boog, Jim thinks "great, an easy play to get the boys off to a good start." Unfortunately, little Boog misses the perfect throw from the second baseman. In fact, he misses the ball completely and it bounces off his chest.

After two kids strike out, the fourth batter in the inning hits a ground ball directly to little Boog. Jim happily rises from his seat to grab a burger from the concession stand before the bottom of the first. But, when little Boog boots the easy grounder, Jim sits back down in frustration. Knowing that the first baseman at this level has to be one of the two or three kids on the team who can catch the ball (or else the team has virtually no chance of getting outs), Jim thinks to himself, "oh poor kid, he must have the opening day jitters."

Five batters and three runs later, Billy's team finally gets the third out. Jim rushes to get his burger, and when he returns to the stands just in time for the lead-off hitter, he yells "okay boys we'll get those runs back."

As luck would have it, Billy's team gets a little rally going when the third batter hits a double. This sets up a good opportunity for the team's cleanup batter to drive in a run. As Jim looks towards the field, he sees a chunky kid lumbering to the plate. When the dust clears, Jim realizes that little Boog is the cleanup hitter as well as the first baseman. After little Boog strikes out on three pitches, Jim wonders why the kid was selected for both of those key spots as it has become obvious by this time that he has no talent whatsoever.

As Jim ponders this question, he glances over to the dugout and notices that the coach of Billy's team also resembles ole Boog Powell, only fatter. Frantically, Jim turns to his wife, Laurie, to confirm his worst fears, and she does – *little Boog's dad is the coach.*

Jim is immediately hit with a flashback from his last season playing little league baseball. During that awful year, the coach's sucky kid pitched or played shortstop every single game. Jim, on the other hand, was relegated to right field, even though it was so obvious that he was one of the best players on the team. Yes, when Jim thought about that painful time, he had to acknowledge that he batted only .185 for the season. However, there was a reason for his slump. It was because he lost his confidence when the manager failed to stick with him. Clearly, Jim recalls, the manager only cared about propping up his own kid, and did not even try to develop the great talent that Jim possessed. As Jim has always pointed out to Laurie when he tells the story of this unjust treatment, Mays was hitless in 25 of his first 26 at bats, but Durocher didn't quit on him. Hell, Jim thinks for the millionth time, *he* could have been the next Mays if he wasn't robbed of the chance by an ignorant coach who couldn't care less about him.

Now Jim's greatest fear was developing right before his own eyes, little Billy was about to suffer through the cruel conse-quences of little league nepotism just as Jim did so many years ago. Game after game, little Boog plays first base and bats clean-up, and game after game he stinks up the field. After about two or three games, Jim has a hushed pre-game talk with another dad wherein he vents his anger over the unvarnished coach bias that is ruining his kid's life. In the weeks that follow, other dads drop lines about little Boog's ineptitude. About halfway through the season, it is obvious to all the parents that little Boog is an awful player and is getting preferential treatment from his dad. Jim is obsessed by this season long crime and wants to take action.

But what can Jim do about it? Jim considers confronting big Boog after a game, but Jim doesn't really like confrontations, especially public ones. Jim also considers complaining to the league president, but he learns that the president is none other than big Boog himself.

Reality sets in. Jim sees that the system is rigged against him. He knows he'll never defeat big Boog's Tammany Hall like bureaucracy and he feels powerless and weak. As Jim walks from the field after Billy's last game, he remembers what his dad told him after Jim complained that only his coach's son got to play shortstop – "Jimmy, you can't fight City Hall, you just can't fight 'em. They'll getcha every time."

Does this scene sound familiar to you? Well, if you have been around kids sports for any significant period of time, you or someone you know has been faced with the same dilemma poor Jim faced. Can the problem be solved you ask?

The answer is no. Just like death and taxes, Coach Dad nepotism is inevitable. There are two reasons for this. First, the vast majority of teams have a dad coach because the dads are usually the only ones in town who will do the job. Other adults don't have the time or incentive to volunteer for a kids coach gig.

Second, it is simply impossible for a parent to coach his kid in a completely objective manner. The late, great basketball coach Al Maguire summarized it best in response to criticism that his son Allie didn't deserve to start on his highly ranked 1971 Marquette team when he said: "I can't be a hypocrite. If my son and another kid are about equal, my son gets the break. Am I operating from intelligence? No, I'm doing it for love."

So all you parents out there who think your kid isn't getting a fair shake this season, you can only solve your problem by becoming part of the problem. Sign up for a coaching job next season and make your klutzy kid the shortstop and cleanup hitter. Sure, the parents of kids who can actually field ground balls are going to be pissed off. But you won't hear their grandstand grumbling – you'll be in the dugout out of ear shot getting the last laugh.

CHAPTER 3

SIDELINE CONVERSATION SCENE I: PC PRESIDENT AND PC TEAM MOM

Preston: Hello Meredith, so glad to see you. I've been meaning to touch base with you to finalize our plans for next year's soccer season.

Meredith: Oh, hello Preston. Of course, how can I help?

Preston: First, I'd like to just thank you for finishing the approved snack list. The rice cakes and vegetable sticks were a great touch.

Meredith: Thanks Preston. As you know, one of my goals is to stop snacking altogether.

Preston: A noble goal, a noble goal indeed. With the way things are in the world, our kids really don't deserve to snack do they. Do you have any thoughts on our cheering rules?

Meredith: Well, I have one potential new rule I've been mulling over. Let me see what you think.

Preston: Okay, let's hear it.

Meredith: Here it is – Parents can only cheer for the kids on the other team.

Preston: So parents can never cheer for their own kids?

Meredith: Yes, and they are required to cheer for the kids on the other team throughout the entire game. You see, our kids will never learn to think about how other people feel unless we teach their parents the concept first.

Preston: That's brilliant Meredith. But, let me see, that means the kids on our travel teams will have nobody cheering for them at all. The parents of the kids from the other towns will cheer their kids on as usual, and our parents will join them. Won't that be an unfair burden on our kids?

Meredith: Unfair? Absolutely not, what's unfair is that some kids get cut from our travel teams. Those are the kids that feel real pain and humiliation after being told by some coach that they are not good enough. With the new rule, the travel team kids will learn what it feels like to be unwanted.

Preston: I see, every game will feel like an away game to them.

Meredith: Yes, which means that our team will lose more games, which will in turn make more kids from other towns feel good about themselves, which will in turn mean that our town will be contributing to the emotional wellbeing of kids throughout the entire county, not just our little town.

Preston: Genius Meredith, pure genius. What a concept, yes, the primary purpose of our league should really be to uplift and care for kids from *other* towns. Yes, because our kids really have it too good in life, you know, living in big houses and all. You're right, our kids simply don't deserve to win soccer games do they. Wow, Meredith you're amazing.

Meredith: Thanks Preston, I appreciate that. I have just one more concept I want to tell you about – a rule for keeping score in the house league.

Preston: Okay, what do you have on that issue?

Meredith: I tell you Preston, I've given this concept of winning and losing a lot of thought, and the emphasis really needs to be rearranged. So what I recommend is a point system that goes like this. Whenever a game is tied, you know when each team scores the same amount of goals, they each get two points. And whenever one team scores more goals than the other, the team with fewer goals gets one point, and the team with more goals gets no points.

Preston: I'm not sure if I get this Meredith.

Meredith: It's that all people, including kids on soccer teams, should try to be equal. So the ultimate goal should be a tie, there's no winners and losers, we're all the same.

Preston: Once again brilliant Meredith, simply brilliant. Equality, that's what sports are really all about. We need to convey that message to the kids. But you know, as I think this out, what would probably happen at first is the kids on teams that are winning games will let the other team score goals so their team can get two points for a tie. But eventually, some of the more competitive kids will figure out that the best strategy is to lose because the losing team gets one point, while the winning team gets no points.

Meredith: That's exactly what I want – we will correct the thought process of these overly competitive kids. Those kids will be incentivized to give up goal after goal to the other team so they can win. And after years and years of this, they will understand that in order to win in life one should really try to lose so other people can feel good about themselves. This attitude makes for a much happier culture don't you think Preston?

Preston: Absolutely Meredith, absolutely. Your concept makes so much sense – in order to learn how to win in life, kids must be conditioned to try their best to lose. You must come to our next meeting to present your ideas to the board. It's Wednesday at 8 pm.

Meredith: I'd be honored. I'll see you there.

CHAPTER 4

STACKING SCHEMES

Virtually every house league has draft rules in place that are meant to balance the teams. Yet, most seasons there are one or two teams that dominate the league, that kick the asses of the little children on the other teams. How does this happen despite the best laid plans? Are the coaches of these dominant teams that good?

While good coaching can make a difference, it alone does not cause domination. No, it's the players stupid, it's the players. As Lou Carnesecca, the legendary St. John's University basketball coach once said when describing a coach's chances for success: "The number one thing, though, he needs to have good players. That's what has to happen first, before anything, if you don't have good players, you're not going to be a good coach."

But how do coaches of dominant teams get so many good players on their rosters? Answer – they are plotting, plotting all off season to come up with scams to get around the draft rules. Here are a few of the classic schemes that coaches utilize to beat the system and stack their teams.

THE ASSISTANT COACH APPOINTMENT SCHEME

The oldest trick in the kids sports stacking book is the old "Assistant Coach Appointment Scheme" by which the head coach selects an assistant coach before the draft whose kid is a superior athlete.

It works as follows – weeks before the draft, the head coach, whose son is a star player, identifies the best players in the league, and asks the dad of one of them to be his assistant coach. Then, on draft day, pursuant to league rules, the head coach's son and the assistant coach's son are automatically placed on the team headed up by those two coaches. This plot gives the head coach a great start by securing at least two top players for his team before draft day. The head coach then only needs to select one or two more good players during the draft to give him a winning team. Some leagues allow head coaches to appoint two assistant coaches, which gives schemers the opportunity to lock up *three* stud players for the roster, and thereby practically guarantee a championship.

Other leagues, including one basketball league I coached in, don't even bother to hold a draft. Instead, they allow coaches to submit their roster to the league. With no rules in place to balance teams in those leagues, there are inevitably one or two shark coaches who secure a star studded roster by recruiting players in the off-season. The other coaches, who naïvely believe that kids sports is only about the kids having fun, fill their rosters with their kids' friends (yes, even the ones that suck). As you would expect, the naïve dudes end up with crappy teams that get blown out by the stacked ones.

After complaining for years about such unethical stacking scams, one year I sold my soul to the devil and tried to implement my own scheme. In my defense, it was not premeditated. It came to me one winter afternoon as I was walking off a gym floor after an indoor lacrosse game next to the dad of a star athlete, a third grader named Kevin. I had coached Kevin in the third/fourth grade basketball league that had just ended. We were only an average team that year because my two best players, Kevin, and my son Ryan, were only third graders.

As I walked beside Kevin's dad it came to me in a flash – if I could get Kevin on my team the following year, he and Ryan, who would then be physically superior fourth graders, could dominate the league. I hesitated for a second, just as the ole Big Dog probably did when Ms. Lewinsky crossed his path in the White House corridors. Sure it didn't feel quite right, but nevertheless, I popped the question to the dad. When the dad said yes, I was overwhelmed by a feeling of joy and elation. I would now, finally, get mine after all those years of doing the right thing and making it all about the kids.

As that third/fourth grade basketball season approached, Ryan and I gloated about the way we would dominate the other children. About a week before the draft, I notified the league president that Kevin's dad would be my assistant coach, and all seemed right with the world. In fact, I never felt better.

Then, it all came crashing down. The league president issued a public edict (*i.e.*, e-mail) to all the coaches notifying them that he had barred Kevin's dad and me from coaching together because Kevin and Ryan were both rated as first round picks. Moreover, the president had the balls to say in his rejection email that his decision was in support of his effort to get the best results for "all" the kids in the program. Talk about bad

65

luck, the one time I tried to play the system I got stuck with a president who was actually on top of things and annoyingly looking out for "all" the kids.

And as if that didn't suck enough, my family ridiculed me for weeks for my hypocritical stacking scheme. While the ridicule was annoying, I had no difficulty weathering it at the time because I had the prize of coaching Kevin and Ryan together awaiting me when the season started. But once the long awaited prize had been taken from me, I felt ripped off. I mean, when Joe Boyd sold his soul to the devil in *Damn Yankees*, at least he got to hit a few homers. In contrast, I got nothing for giving up my fairness principles, not even one measly win led by the fourth grade dynamic duo I had dreamed of.

AGE SCAMS

Have you ever gone to your 12 year old son's game and noticed that the kids on the other team were twice his size and hairier than Robin Williams? If so, your son's team may have been the victim of an age fraud.

The odds of pulling off these scams would seem to be much lower in a house league situation where the kids and families that participate tend to know each other from school, church and other community activities. In fact, the most famous age scam was pulled off in a travel league by Danny Almonte, the Bronx, New York "little leaguer" who struck out 62 of the 72 batters he faced in the 2001 Little League World Series. When suspicious opposing coaches demanded an investigation, it was discovered that Almonte was 14 years old, two years over the league age maximum.

The most troubling aspect of these scams is that they can only be pulled off with the help of a parent and/or coach, who must provide the league with a fake birth certificate. As Jerry Seinfeld is fond of saying, "Who are these people?" I'll tell you Jerry, they are small, very small, sick people. I'm sorry, I've done a few things I regret over the years, but forging a birth certificate so you're 14 year old kid can hit a homer or two off an 11 year old is warped, just plain warped.

Since the Almonte situation, the leagues that my kids have played in have been vigilant about collecting birth certificates from all the players. But no rule or law can stop crooks from hatching ways to get around them. For example, I remember being astonished at the size of several kids on a team that Joe played against in a middle school age AAU basketball league. These kids were huge and they were as skilled as many high school players. Joe's team got blown out by about 70 points. There was simply no way all those kids were 12 or 13 years old – it just didn't look right. So keep your eyes open out there. If it walks like a duck and talks like a duck, it's most likely a duck – a much older than league age duck that is.

THE THROW THE EVALUATION BOONDOGGLE

Many house leagues have a practice of evaluating and ranking all the players before the season starts to provide a mechanism by which balanced teams may be selected. The rankings are provided to the coaches, who then, in theory, should pick the highest ranked players as they proceed through the draft.

However, all the evaluation systems that I've seen have been flawed because they provide too small a sample. For example, the house basketball evaluations I've participated in have generally required each kid to take two full court layups, take two foul shots and participate in short dribbling and passing drills, all of which takes about 90 seconds.

These short evaluations tend to identify only the kids on both extremes – the highly skilled ones and the spazzes. The rest of the kids all seem to have mediocre skills that can't be distinguished during the allocated 90 seconds. Consequently, the rankings for these kids are usually not dependable.

With this scenario, the coaches that draft well are those who have seen a large percentage of the kids play other sports, and therefore, have the scoop on the kid's attitude, coachability and overall athleticism. In other words, they have a much larger evaluation sample than the 90 seconds or so that the league provides.

It is this type of inside information that provides an opportunity for a "Throw the Evaluation Boondoggle." This scam begins when an elite player purposely flubs his 90 second evaluation to obtain an inaccurate low ranking. An "in the know" coach is then able to wait until the late rounds to pick the kid, and select other good players in the early rounds, which guarantees the coach a strong team.

Now, I do not personally know of a kid who was caught flubbing his evaluation to skew a draft ranking. However, I've heard several coaches state their belief that it does in fact happen, and I know of many instances where good players have been given low rankings. Therefore, while I don't have actual proof of any Throw the Evaluation Boondoggles, several of them seem to have happened before my very eyes. Of course, I'm convinced that Oswald conspired with space aliens to kill JFK. So you'll have to take my evaluation conspiracy theory with a grain of salt.

THE NEW KID IN TOWN SCAM

Opportunities for this scam arise when a new, talented athlete moves into town during the season. In this situation, the right thing to do is schedule an evaluation of the kid that all the coaches in the league can observe, and then place him on one of the weaker teams. In contrast to this above board method of team assignment, a "New Kid in Town Scam" occurs when a league official places a new star player on a team, most likely his own, during the middle of the season without giving all the coaches an opportunity to evaluate him.

Of course, once the new kid starts jacking homers or knocking down threes, the scammer will get heat from the coaches who were left out of the loop. However, at that point, with the kid already striking up friendships with new teammates, such scams can easily be closed out by a "It's in the best interest of the child" type of argument. Not that I've ever pulled off one of these scams or anything, but all the scammer has to do is emphasize how horrifically "cruel" it would be to put the child on a different team when he is just starting to feel comfortable in his brand new town. Any league official who couldn't come up with this politician 101 type of "I feel your child's pain" argument just wouldn't deserve the office.

CHAPTER 5
THE DCD QUIZ

When a dad makes the decision to step into the ring and become a coach, he transforms into a public figure in the nature of a politician. Like the politician, the Coach Dad wields a great deal of power, and his decisions, such as the selection of "starting" teams and all-star teams, can have a lasting impact upon the general public, in this case the kids and the parents.

As such, Coach Dads are the regular subject of gossip sessions among parents and kids. Parents will criticize them at house parties for such things as switching pitchers in the sixth inning, sticking with a man-to-man defense against a quicker team, or failing to give them sufficient email notice of practices. Hell, I've even heard kids declare that their coach is "stupid" when they disagree with his strategies.

Like any public figure, the Coach Dad gives up a certain amount of privacy in exchange for the notoriety he has obtained. Once he takes that first step onto the field on opening day, and thereby announces himself as a man of importance, his trips to the market and the hardware store will no longer be anonymous. On the positive side, he will have the pleasure of running into the parents of his star players, who adore him for recognizing their kids' true talents. On the negative side, the Coach Dad will also have to endure such things as the impromptu

Starbucks exchange with the father of a kid he cut from a travel team.

But a dad's decision to become a public figure by coaching little kids, doesn't just affect his status in his local community. No, once the dad steps into the fray, his wife and family are seen in the light created by the dad's behavior. For the most part, the family is not at risk if the dad is just your run of the mill Coach Dad, who struggles through seasons in a good natured way. These type of guys cause no harm. But what if the dad has turned into a DCD or Evil Coach Dad? In such cases, the risk of family embarrassment can be great.

If you believe your dad or husband is on the brink of calling a 9 year old leftfielder a "choker," take the below quiz ASAP, which will diagnose whether or not you need to get him out of coaching to avoid permanent damage to the family's reputation.

We've broken up the types of coaches that the quiz identifies into four categories based on the amount of points that are awarded, as indicated below (please note that "no" answers are zero points).

39 points and above: Scary DCD, a coach who is at risk of exploding at any sporting event he coaches.

26-38 points: Standard DCD, not dangerous, but a coach who delusionally believes coaching T-Ball somehow makes him a real coach.

13-25 points: Borderline DCD, a coach on the brink of attaining the embarrassing DCD status.

0-12 points: Regular Coach Dad, a regular dad who's just in it to have fun.

THE DCD QUIZ

1. Does he constantly wear sweatpants, league or team sweatshirts and jackets, *Under Armour* clothes, "Coach" shirts or other "Coach" outfits? (3 points)

2. Has he ever worn cleats while coaching? (3 points)

3. Does he like Bobby Knight or refer to him or his coaching practices in a positive light while coaching kids? (1 point)

4. Does he brood after a loss by his team? (2 points)

5. Has he risked losing his job by cutting out early so he can make his team's practices and/or games? (3 points)

6. Does he yell at his players on a regular basis? (3 points)

7. Has he ever made a kid cry while coaching? (3 points)

8. Has he ever cried while coaching or talking about his team? (2 points)

9. Does he often refer to his high school, college, or kids league sports exploits? (2 points; add 2 more points if the stories aren't even true)

10. Have you observed him reviewing his high school year book sports section more than once? (2 points)

11. Does he yell at umpires or referees on a regular basis? (3 points)

12. Does he break out the booze after big wins? (1 point)

13. Does he break out the booze after big losses? (1 point)

14. Has he argued with an opposing coach more than once? (3 points)

15. Has he expressed the view that kids leagues should not have minimum play requirements? (3 points)

16. Does he ignore minimum play rules while coaching? (5 points)

17. Has he ever been involved in an Assistant Coach Appointment Scheme or other stacking scam? (3 points)

18. Has he ever scouted the opposing teams in a league for kids under 10 years old? (2 points)

19. Has he expressed the view that travel teams should start when kids are 8 or under? (3 points)

20. Does he carry a clipboard containing his coaching materials on a semi-regular basis? (2 points)

21. Does he refer to non-athletic kids on his team as "spazzes" or some other derogatory name? (5 points)

22. Does he forget the names of the "bench players" on his team? (2 points)

23. Does he think his kid will be a pro or D1 college player? (3 points)

24. Does he study video or film of his team's games? (4 points)

25. Is his family spending more money than it can reasonably afford on youth sports activities at his insistence? (4 points)

26. Has he ever been ejected from a game while coaching kids? (10 points)

CHAPTER 6

HIGH SCHOOL REVISITED/KIDS SPORTS CLASS WARFARE

Ah, I can see it now, 1979, St. John the Baptist High School in West Islip, New York. Like every other high school, we had numerous cliques. Our pop culture tells us that jocks, cheerleaders and rich kids top the social hierarchy in U.S. high schools. At least that's what the creators of productions such as *16 Candles, The Breakfast Club, Beverly Hills 90210* and *American Pie* seem to think. My high school was a little different in that the partiers, rich kids, and kids who could otherwise project coolness comprised the elite group. Playing on a school team or cheerleading would not by itself include you among the elites, although it scored you extra points if you were otherwise within that group.

Moving forward 30 years or so, I have noted that, just like high school, the sports parent society has a very clear social hierarchy. In fact, us parents take on roles that are analogous to the roles that kids play in high school.

HIGH SCHOOL JOCK = COACH DAD

In most high schools, the jocks have it made. They play games before large crowds of students; they constantly demand attention by wearing their team jackets and other jock wear in the halls of the school; they get the local press coverage; they date the hot chicks; and they sit at the cool jock table in the cafeteria. As a result of this high visibility and standing, the jocks are in a clear position of power within the high school social structure.

In the sports parent culture, the Coach Dads hold the high visibility, high power positions that put them at the top of the sports parent social ladder. Just like high school jocks, the Coach Dads ostentatiously announce their high place in the local society by prancing around town in their team jackets, sweatshirts and other sports get-ups. And they wield a great deal of power as the deciders of which kids play the star positions, which kids ride the pine, and which kids are selected for travel teams. As a result of this visible power, some parents kiss up to the Coach Dads just like some out of the cool loop kids kiss up to the high school jocks – it's downright sickening.

RICH HIGH SCHOOL KIDS = PSPs

In the kids sports culture, parents of star players ("PSPs") are also part of the cool crowd. Just like the high school rich kid, the PSP is blessed with an enviable type of wealth, a kick-ass athlete who can be seen by the neighbors. And boy do the PSPs get a lot of attention from their athletic spawn. Shallow parents fawn all over them in the same way that shallow high school girls suddenly "like" the nerdy dudes who show up driving BMWs on the first day of eleventh grade. But beware you PSPs out there, you will swiftly drop out of the elite parent category if your kid becomes a mere mediocre player.

NOBODIES = PARENTS OF BENCHWARMERS

The Merriam Webster Online Dictionary defines a "nobody" as "a person of no influence or consequence." In high school, the nobodies are the faceless, nameless kids who never become "known" because they are not included in any of the power groups or cliques. As a result, they are "of no consequence" to the high school social scene.

In the sports parent culture, the parents of the benchwarmers are the nobodies. Sadly, it's an unavoidable fact that if your kid rides the pine, some parents won't take the time to get to know you or your kid. In contrast, if your kid makes a few good plays, other parents will make a point of meeting you as part of the process of establishing the social hierarchy for that season. This process can be observed during games when parents ask "Who scored that goal?", "Who had that hit?" or "Who made that catch?", etc. If your kid is never the answer to those questions, the shallow parent types won't give a crap who you are.

GIRL EVENT ORGANIZERS = TEAM MOM/MANAGER

I'm sure ya'll remember the girls back in high school who annoyingly organized the big events (prom, homecoming, etc.) while everyone else was goofing off like teenagers are supposed to do. In the kids sports scene, the Team Moms take on the analogous role of organizing games and practices, and guiding parents through the web of responsibilities they must meet during the season.

CHEERLEADER = CHEERLEADING COACH

The whole concept of cheerleading – girls performing panty-showing cartwheels as a sideshow to boys games has become politically incorrect in much of the northeast (where I live). Consequently, I haven't heard many moms boast about their high school cheerleading days. The exception to this trend are the mom cheerleading coaches I've met, many of whom proudly wear their cheerleading jackets and work hard to pass on the cheerleading tradition to their daughters. I picture these women as the one or two cheerleaders on their high school squads who actually bought into the concept of cheering their school teams on to victory, as opposed to the ones who sought status by joining up. While such status seekers move on to new symbols of success as adults, such as joining the "right" country club or taking up the latest trendy cause, the moms who volunteer their time to coach cheerleading in this day and age have remained true to their passion – ya gotta respect that.

THE HAVES v. THE HAVE-NOTS

To use the parlance of Karl Marx, the high school society is comprised of social "Haves" and "Have-Nots." The Haves are the in, cool kids (historically the jocks, cheerleaders and rich kids). And the Have-Nots are the nerds and nobodies, who are excluded from the cool parties, the cool tables in the cafeteria, and the cool kid hang-outs around town. The Have-Nots who attempt to break into the top tier of the high school society are typically rejected by the Haves and forced to return to their proletariat origins.

Similarly, in the sports parent culture, there is an ever present Haves vs. Have-Nots class struggle. The Haves are the parents of "travel" or "all-star" team players, many of whom are also coaches, assistant coaches and league officers. The Have-Nots are all the remaining parents.

The Haves begin the process of establishing their superiority over the Have-Nots when their kids start playing organized sports at the age of 4 or 5. The dads volunteer as coaches, and the moms volunteer as team managers and fundraiser types. The dads then coach teams in the house leagues for two or three years, and establish their kids' reputations as "star" players by playing them at the high exposure positions and developing their skills during extra practice sessions.

All this preparation sets these parents up for the time when the bright line between the Haves and the Have-Nots is firmly drawn – when the first "travel" team is selected in the particular sport.

The children of the coach Have types enjoy a huge advantage over the other kids when this time comes. Most importantly, the coaches know that there are such things as travel teams for kids as young as 7 or 8, and find out when and where these tryouts are held. This "insider" knowledge gives the coaches the opportunity to train their kids for the try-outs. In contrast, the less focused parents do not take the time to prepare their kids for these events. And some parents fail to even get their kids to travel team try-outs because they concentrate on things that actually matter, such as their kids' education and overall intellectual development. Not surprisingly given this scenario, the children of the well-prepared parents are normally selected for travel teams, which propels the parents into the Have sector.

With few exceptions, the kids who remain interested in the subject sport become the "anointed" travel team players until high school. This travel team tenure firmly establishes their parents' standing within the Have community for those years, far above the Have-Not parents, who have bred mere house players.

What benefits do the Haves enjoy during their time within that high status group? Their kids assimilate easily because their place on a travel team gives them respect in the kid community. They have a basis for believing that their kids will be offered a college athletic scholarship in a few more years. They get to go to "cool" parties thrown by other Haves. They get to announce their family's "A List" status by purchasing travel team jackets, sweatshirts and caps for their kids to wear around town. But most of all, the more insecure Haves get to repeatedly declare their superiority over the Have-Not parents by dropping the term "travel" during conversations with them in a condescending tone (*i.e.*, "Billy has a 'travel' soccer game tomorrow, we're leaving for Boston at 6 a.m.").

Is it possible for a Have-Not parent to break into the Have crowd by virtue of his or her kid making a travel team in its second season or afterwards? The answer is yes, but it is difficult. In my experience, most of the kids selected to the first travel team for a given sport (usually in fifth or sixth grade or so) deserve it because their interested parents have given them a good head start. However, as the years pass, other kids catch up to some of the anointed ones when they develop skills or become physically superior. While some of these outsiders will eventually deserve to make the travel team based on talent and/or skills alone, there are often political factors that limit the amount of open spots on the roster.

For example, all the coaches' kids have locked up spots even if they don't deserve them, and some kids who were previously among the best players maintain their spots by reputation. You see, these travel teams tend to become insular communities comprised of coaches, parents and kids that become almost like family. As such, coaches are sometimes not open to recognizing the talents of outsiders. With these factors at play, the only kids who tend to break onto travel team rosters in later years, and thereby propel their parents into the Haves stratosphere, are those who clearly rank as one of the top four or five players on the particular travel team.

So what is the lesson here? What can a parent do to secure a spot within the Haves culture if that is a goal? Answer – you must follow the FIFO method of sports parenting – First In, First On. Become a coach of a house team from day one (years before any travel team is selected), and volunteer for league officer positions. As the coach of a house team, you should maintain friendly relationships with the other house coaches, one of whom will most likely become the first travel coach for that age group. Through all of this involvement, your kid will be a known entity before the first travel team tryout, and will most likely make the team as long as he or she is moderately talented. Of course, you can *guarantee* a place on the team for your child by utilizing the FIFO method to lobby for, and obtain, the travel team head coach or assistant coach job.

CHAPTER 7

THE "OTHER PARENTS" GAME

When your kid plays on a team, there are a group of people that you can't avoid no matter how hard you try – the parents of the other kids on the team (the "Other Parents"). Initially, you'll see them at just the obvious places, the practices and games. But, soon enough, you'll run into Other Parents at alternate locations, away from the field. One week, it's the market, and the next week it's the post office. By mid-season, the off the field Other Parent encounters will increase to two, even three times a week, and it becomes clear that these folks are now part of your life, until the end of the season any way.

Indeed, Other Parent relationships can become quite complex. The parents of kids on the same team go through many emotional highs and lows together during any one season. Each parent will see his or her child experience painful public failures, such as striking out to end the game or missing a key foul shot. And together, these parents will celebrate the big wins and lament the overtime losses.

I've been lucky, the vast majority of the Other Parents I've known over the years have been nice folks. But you can't help but run into a few bad apples. For example, when I was one of two assistant coaches of Joe's baseball team one year, I had to regularly deal with an angry, bitter parent. The other assistant coach was a surly man named Brian, who was infuriated when the head coach, Ken, made Joe the first pitcher and starting first baseman over Brian's son, John. Trust me folks, this was not a borderline situation. Joe was tall and had advanced skills, while John was short and had hands of stone.

Even though Ken picked the line-up for each game, Brian took out his frustration on me. He would ignore my happy hellos as I arrived on the field and walk away when I tried to join conferences that he and Ken were holding. When we were forced into conversations by unavoidable consequences, Brian would snort out short, terse responses to my attempts at light-hearted banter. The pained look on Brian's face during those brief encounters told the whole story – he hated my guts!!

So how do you develop sane parent relationships, avoid the Brians of the world, and win the Other Parents Game? Answer – follow my six essential rules of parent relationships.

1. *Utilize the Dale Carnegie Sideline Conversation Philosophy.* If you've been in the kids sports scene for a while like I have, you know that parents go to games for just one reason – to see *their* kids play. Sure, they'd prefer that the team win the game. But the team's success is a side issue for the sports parent. With few exceptions, such as the Important Businessman and the I Don't Give A Crap Parent, when the kid is playing well, the parent is happy, and when the kid is playing badly, the parent is miserable. It's as simple as that.

Given this reality, parents can get off to a great start to a season by following three of Dale Carnegie's famous *Golden Rules on How to Win Friends and Influence People*: (i) be a good listener, encourage others to talk about themselves; (ii) talk in terms of the other person's interests; and (iii) remember that a person's name is to that person the sweetest and most important sound in any language. Practically speaking, this means that parents can, and will earn a spot in the "cool" part of the stands by learning the names of the Other Parents and their kids; using these names repeatedly in conversation; encouraging Other Parents to talk about the most important thing in their lives, their offspring; and taking the pain while Other Parents ramble on endlessly about their child's on the field trials and tribulations.

Conversely, boaster types who dominate every conversation with anecdotes about his/her kid's travel team exploits do not mix well with Other Parents. By mid-season, the Other Parents figure these egocentric bores out, and sit as far away from them as possible.

See the following example of two conversations between Lillian and Nora, parents of 9 year old little leaguers, demonstrating how to, and how not to, win Other Parent friends.

THE GOOD WAY

Lillian: Hey Nora, Brian really looks quick out there. He's in such great condition.

Nora: Oh thanks Lillian, you're so nice. He's down to 185 pounds.

Lillian: If one of the kids ever hits the ball all the way into right field, I'm sure Brian would catch it.

Nora: You're so sweet, let's grab a cup of coffee after the game.

THE BAD WAY

Lillian: Sorry we're late, Kyle had a tryout for the travel team. The coach called us Friday night and told us to make sure Kyle was there.

Nora: Really…

Lillian: Either Kyle or Jimmy Simmons will be the starting shortstop. But we ran into Dan Meehan, you know the league president, and he said that Kyle will definitely get it.

Nora: I have to go to the bathroom.

2. Drive, Drive, Drive. Driving the kids to and from their games and practices is the primary responsibility parents have during any given season. The task can become very time consuming, especially if the kid is on a travel team that plays games in far away towns. So, one of the best ways to create good will is to drive Other Parents' kids to their events. This helps working parents avoid the risk of leaving the job early to make a weekday game, and gives the stay at home parent free time for something fun, like an afternoon at the gym. At worst, the Other Parent will turn down the offer, but think positive thoughts about the "generous" parent who offered to drive.

In order to maximize the impact of the Drive, Drive, Drive strategy, I recommend paying your dues early in the season. You will then be ahead of the game, and can cash in chips to obtain rides for your kid late in the season, when many parents are sick and tired of going to ball games.

However, parents beware. If you utilize this driving strategy, there is one big pitfall – don't be late. This is especially important if your child is on a travel team where some coaches punish kids for tardiness. If you are the reason an Other Parent's kid loses his starting point guard spot, your entire strategy will have backfired, and you will be reviled by the parent you sought to impress.

3. *Never Publicly Criticize Another Parent's Kid.* Picture this scene. Ralph Cameron spots Lynn Fanning in the frozen foods aisle, and recalls that after Lynn's son, little Billy Fanning, struck out looking to end the last game, Ralph yelled out in frustration: "shit Billy, be a hitter, not looker." Further, Ralph recalls that as he walked from the field he saw Billy crying in his mother's arms.

As Ralph closes to just ten feet from Lynn, he is scared to death that Lynn will spot him and admonish him for hurting her little boy. So Ralph quickly u-turns his cart to avoid eye contact with Lynn, and scampers out of the aisle. While Ralph makes it out of the market unscathed, in the subsequent days he tells his wife that he doesn't think he can make it to the Fanning's annual Memorial Day barbecue. He also internally debates whether he should sit on the opposing team's side of the field the rest of the season to avoid awkward conversations with Lynn. As these things run through his mind, Ralph thinks to himself, "How the hell did I get myself into this mess?" Answer – breaking Rule #3, never publicly criticize another parent's kid.

This is just common sense people. No parent wants to hear a dickhead three seats to his right scream at his kid for missing the cut-off man or failing to box-out an opposing player. I repeatedly experienced this offensive conduct during a particular basketball season several years ago and it pissed me off to no end. Needless to say, I don't hang with the dude who was yelling at my son.

Bottom line, if one of the little 10 year olds on your kid's team makes a bad play, keep it to yourself on the field, and whine about it to your spouse at home. That way, the kid will avoid unnecessary embarrassment and his parents won't hate you.

4. *Cover Parent Assignments.* Most every kids sport season begins with a speech from the coach in which he will go on about how he wants the kids to learn the fundamentals of the game, play together as a team, and most of all just have fun. And then towards the end of the speech, the coach will say that running the squad is a "team" effort, and he expects all the parents to help with necessary tasks, such as operating the scoreboard, maintaining the field, running the concession stand, keeping the scorebook, and providing the team snack. A couple of my kids' coaches have even gone as far as to send a schedule identifying the dates that each parent was "required" to perform an assigned task.

Being both a coach and sports parent for many years, I've been on both ends of these speeches. And believe me, most parents, including me, avoid these jobs like the plague.

And for good reason, most of them really suck. For example, operating a basketball game scoreboard is a high stress job – a close game could be won or lost by the parent's screw-up. More importantly, when parents take on such a job, they are deprived of the one reason they came to the game, which is to watch their kid play ball. They can't do this while they're working the scoreboard because they have to focus on such inane things as when the ball goes out of bounds, and whether the shooter made one or both of his two foul shots.

Therefore, if getting along with Other Parents is a goal, volunteer to do one of the assigned tasks on a regular basis. This will take the pressure off the Other Parents, allow them to sit back and enjoy the game, and at the same time establish your good reputation within the team community.

5. *Utilize the Abstinence Method When Necessary.* During any given season, all parents are at risk of unavoidable annoying Other Parent exposure. Whether it be a Know-It-All Dad, PC Team Mom or one way talker type, conversations with these people can be torture. And when the Know-It-All Dad takes a seat next to you for the fifth game in a row, and he tells you for the thirtieth time that season that the coach is screwing up by not playing a zone defense, you'd just love to tell him to shut the hell up. But can you really do that when your wife is friends with his wife, and you have to see the guy at the team's seven remaining games? Of course not, that will get you into more trouble than the dude is worth.

In such circumstances, you must utilize the "Abstinence Method", and abstain from all contact with the Other Parent to avoid a major blow-up that you will regret. To achieve the best results with this method, you must be well-prepared. You cannot arrive early to the game because you will run the risk of the Other Parent spotting you and grabbing a seat next to you. Instead, arrive a little late so you can determine where the Other Parent is sitting. Once you've done that, quickly move far away from his game viewing location. For example, if he's in the stands, go to a standing spot along the field. If he's standing along the first base line, go to the stands behind the backstop, etc. However, don't get cocky upon achieving your initial safe haven because the dude will wander from his location if he has not found a dad to complain to. Stay focused, keep your eyes on him, and be prepared to bust to a new location if you spot him coming your way.

Granted, applying the Abstinence Method to avoid unwanted parent contact takes a great deal of effort. But unlike the abstinence method of birth control, the thing you're avoiding is no fun at all. And the return on your investment, one less conversation with a blowhard, is well worth it.

6. *Don't Be An Asshole.* "Did you hear what Bill Franklin did at the playoff game on Saturday, what an asshole," "Quick Frank, take the seat next to me, I don't want that asshole Bill Franklin to sit there," "Oh man, I feel sorry for Robby Franklin, it must suck having an asshole for a dad."

How did poor Bill Franklin get into this mess? He ignored one of the life's most basic rules – don't be an asshole man, just don't be an asshole. It's probably the third most important rule, right after brushing your teeth three times a day and tipping your bartender early in the night to guarantee subsequent rounds of free shots.

But what type of behavior warrants an "asshole" label in the kids sports context? Well, an occasional minor transgression won't raise a parent to the asshole level. Most parents understand that watching your kid drop a pop fly, or miss six foul shots in the last 90 seconds of a game, is painful. So we'll give a dad a pass for an isolated holler at the umpire or referee in frustration after his son made a bonehead play.

Rather, a parent will earn the "asshole" designation by a pattern of objectionable conduct during the season. Practically speaking, this means a series of missteps comprised of such things as yelling at umpires or referees; public disagreements with the coaches of the team; registering complaints to the league about the parent's spazzy kid not being a starting player; boasting about his kid's "travel" team exploits; excessive public criticism by the parent of his own kid; blowing driving assignments; never offering to drive kids to practices or games; just being generally rude; and yelling at other parents' kids when they screw up.

However, there are certain types of incidents that are so outrageous that they automatically label the parent as an asshole. For example, any dad who gets kicked out of a gym for excessive complaining to a referee earns the asshole designation for that act alone. Although I've heard many stories of this happening over the years, I've only seen it happen once. The guy made a fool out of himself by repeatedly screaming about the referee's calls in a basketball league played by sixth graders. Luckily, the referee didn't take any guff. He gave the moron a couple of warnings, and when the guy continued, the referee stopped the game until he left the gym.

The most extreme type of behavior that automatically earns a dad asshole status is a physical assault of a coach or referee. Luckily, I've never actually seen this happen. I've only heard stories of such acts of lunacy or read about them in the papers.

At this point, the dad assholes who are reading this book (you know who you are) are probably wondering whether they can ever wipe the slate clean after getting kicked out of a gym or punching a coach in the mouth. I guess it's possible, us Americans are forgiving people. You're best hope is that you were drunk when the incident occurred. First of all, on the positive side, hopefully you had a few laughs while you downed the pre-game brews. But, more practically speaking, I recommend that you blame your ludicrous behavior on the booze; complete a rehab program; and rejoin the community the next season supported by the claim that you are a new man. Hey, it worked for Robert Downey, Jr., so why not you.

The dads who are sober when they throw their first blow at a referee worry me way more than the drunken ones who do. I just can't imagine what type of referee's call could make a dad angry enough to brawl without the help of at least four *Johnnie Walkers*. But hey, as long as the dude doesn't live on my block, I don't want to know.

CHAPTER 8

SIDELINE CONVERSATION SCENE II: DAD OF STARTING POINT GUARD AND DAD OF BACK-UP POINT GUARD, BOTH KNOW-IT-ALL DADS

Bob is the father of Kevin, the starting point guard. Hank is the father of Michael, the back-up point guard.

Hank: [thinking, *Oh damn, here comes that shithead Bob.*] Hey Bob, how's it going?

Bob: [*Oh no, I gotta talk to this guy again?*] Hey what's up Hank?

Hank: [*Kevin is the slowest guard I ever saw.*] Man, Kevin had some game yesterday. He looked like Steve Nash out there.

Bob: [*What's his kid's name again? Oh yeah, Michael.*] How about Michael's dish to Tommy? That was the play of the day.

Hank: [*He sure didn't turn the ball over fifteen times like that little putz Kevin.*] Thanks Bob, I appreciate that.

Bob: [*Must find seat, must escape!*] Oh it's nothing man, I can't wait to see Michael dish a few more today.

Hank: [*Yeah, and I can't wait to see Kevin blow yet another game for us.*] Aw thanks, but Kevin is the kid to watch, he's some ballplayer.

Bob: [*Help, help, help! Where's my damn wife when I need her?*] Thanks Hank. So am I going to see you at the end of the season party next week?

Hank: [*Oh please God no.*] Yeah I hope so.

Bob: [*Oh please God no.*] Okay, I'll see you there.

Hank: [*Later, dickface.*] Great to talk to you Bob. Say hi to Helen for me.

Bob: [*Later, loser.*] No the pleasure was all mine, take care.

CHAPTER 9

THE FORNICATING CATHOLIC SCHOOL BOYS AND OTHER FOOTBALL STORIES

So there I was in August 1974, attending an evening practice of the Blessed Trinity eighth grade football team. The head coach, Mr. Harrelson, was not there for the start of the practice. So our assistant coach, Phil Pisani, was running it.

Approximately one hour into the practice, Harrelson, a stocky man of about 40 years, showed up and walked towards us on the large grass field. We had been told that Harrelson was a good football player in his day, and I always pictured him as a linebacker type playing with one of those helmets with no face mask, like Sid Luckman and Bobby Lane used to do. Harrelson had been coaching Blessed Trinity football teams for several years and had the reputation of a mean, ornery guy. In person, he lived up to it.

As Harrelson came closer to us that day, I started to get nervous as I always did when he came my way. However, as he reached our general area on the field, his gait was noticeably off. In fact, he was wobbling a little bit. As was his way, he immediately started barking out instructions. This time, however, his words came out in a garbled, slurred, indecipherable manner. From my years of watching Dean Martin's act and certain relatives and neighbors, it soon became clear that Harrelson was smashed. But it wasn't the happy kind of drunkenness that Dean always displayed. No, Harrelson was pissed off.

By the time Harrelson fully reached our location on the field, all of us had stopped our football activities to stare in amazement at our drunken head coach. At this point, some of Harrelson's garbled words could be understood. He was calling us in words or substance, the worst possible thing you can call a football team – a bunch of pussies.

To prove our pussiness, Harrelson dropped down into a wobbly three-point stance directly in front of one of my 13 year old teammates, and challenged him to a block-off. When the kid refused to take him on, Harrelson challenged another kid. When that kid also refused to block the drunken head coach, Harrelson went on to yet another kid, who also declined. After about five scared-as-hell kids failed to take Harrelson's bait, Harrelson stepped up to our biggest and best player, Jim McAndrew, who was about six feet tall at the time, and would eventually grow into a 6'4" 230 pound college football star.

As Harrelson ripped into Jimmy with an insult-laden rant, I knew things were going to get even worse. Instead of backing down, Jimmy charged Harrelson and blocked him as hard as he could. I'll never forget the result of that block – Harrelson's false teeth came flying out of his mouth as he slammed to the turf. For a moment, there was silence, but finally Phil (our assistant coach) stopped the madness, picked up the dazed Harrelson and directed him off the field.

As you may imagine, Harrelson's tenure as head coach ended that evening.

With our erstwhile head coach out for the count, Phil took over the job. Phil was about 21 years old, 6'1" and 220 pounds. He told us he had played on a local college football team. I have no memory of how Phil was selected to replace Harrelson. But it soon became apparent that what, if any, vetting process our school utilized was woefully inadequate.

Phil presented himself to us as a kind of wild, fun-loving, jock partier, who brought us 13 year old boys into his world by periodically regaling us with his late night adventures. Thus, our Saturday morning practices would at times begin or end with a story about such things as Phil's shot-slamming drinking escapades from the night before; the bar room brawl that Phil and his buddies had gotten into; or the fine girl that he had recently dated.

One story during that season that still sticks out in my mind was Phil's detailed description of a "blow job" he had received from a young lady that he had come to know. I remember being a little uncomfortable during that speech, especially because I wasn't exactly sure what a blow job was. Oh sure I knew it was some kind of a sex act, I just didn't know what kind. Eventually I figured it out from the context clues and a few hints from other kids.

Phil also enjoyed abusing kids by his warped application of the age old fumble drill. Those of you out there who have played football know that whenever a coach throws a football onto the field and yells "fumble," the players will, without fail, run and dive for the football attempting to "recover it" as if their life depends on it. Well, my man Phil used the fumble drill as a kind of weapon against kids who rubbed him the wrong way. So, for example, if one of our players made a big blunder in practice or said something stupid in Phil's mind, Phil would throw the ball towards him, yell "fumble" and the rest of the players would pile on the poor kid.

As far as I recall, none of our players were ever injured when they were the target of Phil's fumble drill prank. But Phil almost got us all killed when he pulled the prank on an outsider. On that occasion, a kid spectator ridiculed us throughout a practice and claimed that another local football team was far better than ours. Finally, Phil had enough of the little loud mouth, and you guessed it, threw the football toward him and yelled "fumble!" The team, on cue, charged the kid and trampled him much to Phil's delight.

Unfortunately, this move backfired. The next day about 20 of the kids' large and much older friends were waiting for us at the field before the start of our practice, poised to whip our asses. Luckily, most of us spotted the bad guys as we arrived to the park and sped away on our bikes. But one kid and his mom did not escape. The hooligans spotted them as the mom pulled her car up to the field, and proceeded to pound the hell out of it until the mom maneuvered her way out of the jam.

However, out of the many unconventional things that Phil did that year, the thing I remember most is the name he gave our team. The name was derived from a ritual that Harrelson had started before his forced departure. Harrelson would periodically end his speeches to the team by yelling "What is the name of this team?" In response, we would yell, "Blessed Trinity!" If our response was not loud enough, Harrelson would demand one and we would in turn yell even louder, "Blessed Trinity! Blessed Trinity!"

Well, soon after he took over the job, Phil decided that "Blessed Trinity" was no name for a football team. So he came up with a new name that he thought best fit us Catholic school boys – *The Fornicators*. Continuing with Harrelson's tradition, at various points during our practices, Phil would call us together, have each of us put our hand into a circle, and yell, "What's the name of this team?" We would then, very much enjoying our opportunity to yell a vulgar word, yell, "The Fornicators!" Like Harrelson, when Phil felt that we had not shouted out our team name enthusiastically enough, he would demand that we yell it much louder. To which we would all respond with even louder shouts, "The Fornicators! The Fornicators! The Fornicators!"

Of course, Phil was smart enough to keep our chants out of our parents' earshot. And, as far as I know, none of us kids ever revealed any of Phil's antics to our unsuspecting parents – I certainly didn't. Consequently, they never discovered the X-rated education that Phil gave us Catholic school boys during that 1974 season.

Why am I telling ya'll these childhood football anecdotes? To support my view that the typical kids football coach is a more dangerous animal than the guys who normally coach other youth sports. This should come as a surprise to no one given that a primary objective of the sport is to knock the crap out of the players on the other team.

During my fifth through twelfth grade years, I played baseball, basketball, football, and lacrosse, and I was chewed out by men coaching all those sports. While I didn't particularly enjoy those rants, I understood that was part of the deal. If you screwed up, you would be reprimanded, and you just had to figure out a way to do it better the next time. But the football coaches were the only ones who *physically* punished boys when they screwed up with slaps to the helmet, face mask yanks, and kicks to the ass. Even worse, some of these men seemed to enjoy intimidating us little guys.

Since my kids don't play football, I haven't had the opportunity to personally observe any warped football coach antics in recent years. However, press reports of *criminal* acts performed by kids football coaches confirm that nothing has changed over the years. For example, in October 2006, in Oakland, New Jersey, 33 year old coach Erick Marreo was charged with assault for throwing punches during a brawl among coaches, parents and seventh grade players. In November 2001, in Sarasota, Florida, Trevor Harvey, a 34 year old coach, was arrested after he punched the referee during his 7 year old son's flag football game. And in June 2012, Dexter Austin, another Sarasota, Florida football coach, was found guilty of battery for instigating a fight with a referee.

And just look at the many famous football coaches who have proved to be violent, unstable maniacs. One of the most renowned coaches in the history of the sport, Woody Hayes, was fired from his Ohio State job in 1978 for punching an opposing player who had intercepted a pass. More recently, in 2010, former University of South Florida coach, Jim Leavitt, was fired after he allegedly slapped a player twice in the face and then lied about it. And in 2009, Mike Leach was fired from his Texas Tech coaching job after he allegedly locked a player in a dark shed because he was dogging it during practice. With guys like this to look up to, no wonder there are so many crazy kids football coaches out there.

Of course, the vast majority of youth football coaches are good guys. In fact, I count a few of them as friends. Many a youth football coach will tell you that football provides a great forum to teach kids about important attributes that we all need in life, such as discipline, commitment, toughness, teamwork and perseverance. And I buy into that.

When football players lose a game badly, it is, of course, painful for them to watch the other team run across the goal line for touchdown after touchdown. But that is not the worst of it; the losing players also get clobbered all game. Yet, they get up off the grass time after time for the next play, the next battle, with honor. The youth football coaches who are able to instill this type of grit in kids are, undoubtedly, doing them a great service.

Looking back at my childhood football experience, I was, all things considered, pretty lucky. Yes, I had football coaches grab my face mask a couple of times. But I also learned the meaning of the term "blow job" from a football coach. That's the type of practical guidance I just wasn't receiving from my teachers at Blessed Trinity School.

CHAPTER 10

RULES, RULES, RULES

What are the most regulated industries in the United States? Tobacco, oil, banking you say? Well maybe so, but youth sports has got to be way up there. However, it wasn't always that way. When I was a kid, it was like the wild west, man. Coaches played to win. Lousy players rode the pine all damn season. And when boys screwed up, coaches would call them horrible names like "ladies," "pussies," "girls," and "losers."

Parents were, by today's standards, politically incorrect to the extreme. They screamed awful things about opposing players. Dads downed brews on the sidelines, polluted the fresh spring air with cigarette and cigar smoke, and drove kids home buzzed. In fact, stepping through crushed beer cans in the back of a car was a skill I had to master to get through rides from a certain dad I knew.

I don't recall ever hearing of the concept of a "healthy" snack when I was a kid. Snacks were by definition unhealthy. While there was the occasional orange, for the most part, we ate potato chips, candy, soda, and of course, ice cream after the game.

Looking back at all this, I have to say that some regulations were probably in order. But now the pendulum has swung too far to the other side. Today, kids leagues have many, many types of rules including score keeping rules, minimum play require-ments, team selection rules, and coach, spectator and player codes of conduct. And, believe it or not, there are quite a few cities and towns that have enacted real live laws to regulate the sports played by our boys and girls.

Here's a summary of the more prevalent rules to give ya'll an edge over the losers who did not buy my highly insightful book.

SCORE KEEPING RULES

The primary purpose of score keeping rules is to deemphasize the concept of "winning" so kids won't feel bad when they lose. Consistent with this concept, many leagues don't keep score of games played by very young kids, like 4, 5 and 6 year olds. All games end in a tie. I agree with these rules, but as kids get older, certainly by 7 years old, they should understand that the team with more points, runs or goals wins the game and the other team loses it.

Some leagues disagree. For example, as late as 2006-07, the San Francisco Police Activities League ("SFPAL") soccer program had a Coaches/Parent/Spectator Code of Conduct that sought to change the meaning of the term "winner". Under that code, a "winner" did not mean a team who scored more goals than the opposition. Instead, SFPAL instructed parents to "[r]edefine what it means to be a 'Winner' in your conversations with players and other fans" to mean "people who make maximum effort, continue to learn and improve, and do not let mistakes, or fear of making mistakes stop them."

So people, are you getting this? In order to save kids from suffering through a "loss" now and then, SFPAL actually changed the meaning of a term in the English language. But really SFPAL, why stop with soccer? In basketball, a field goal can be redefined as "any shot that hits the rim." In baseball, a "put out" can be redefined to mean "any attempt by a fielder to catch the ball." And while you're at it SFPAL, why don't you just strike the word "out" from the entire baseball rule book. You see where I'm going. I'm sure the SFPAL leadership meant well, but you can't legislate "losses" out of a kid's life.

MINIMUM PLAY REQUIREMENTS

These rules guarantee a certain amount of play time in each game for all players. For example, many baseball leagues require that every kid play at least three innings. Minimum play requirements are most common in house leagues. However, for the record, I believe that such rules should be in place for travel leagues as well because youth sports are by definition developmental. Amazingly, I found one organization, the Thief River Falls Minnesota Backcourt Club, which is proud of the fact that the kids on its *third grade* travel basketball team do not get equal play time. The Club's 2012 rules specifically provide that "[o]ur goal is to win as many tournaments as possible" and "[p]layers will not receive equal playing time."

TRAVEL/ALL-STAR TEAM SELECTION RULES

The selection of travel teams is a consistent area of controversy. There is a limited amount of spots on these teams, and the parents of kids who don't make them often feel the process is unfair. In my experience, there are two issues that parents are reasonably concerned about.

First, the coach usually has a kid trying out, which is an obvious conflict. Second, kids who have played on a previous year's travel team have an advantage over kids who haven't because coaches tend to move up with teams.

For example, it is very common for a coach to start out coaching a sixth grade travel team and continue coaching the same group of kids through eighth grade. In this situation, kids who try out for the first time in seventh or eighth grade have a steep hill to climb. As I explained in Chapter 6, if the new kid would be one of top players on the squad, he's usually got a pretty good shot of making it. In such a case, the coach can justify dumping the worst kid on the previous year's team because the new player will make the team better. But if the new kid is only as good as the last four or five players from the previous year's team, and he therefore would not improve the team, his chances are slim. In that scenario, coaches tend to keep the players they already know over a new kid. In other words, a tie goes to the kid who played on last year's travel team.

Given these common problems, I am in favor of rules that make the selection of travel teams a more fair process. Sure, I know that even with such rules in place abuses occur. But, at the very least, they tend to deter the blatant ones.

Among the typical measures that leagues implement to keep try-outs fair are rules: establishing how try-out dates will be announced (so parents can't claim that they weren't notified about the try-outs); establishing the use of "independent evaluators" to rate the kids; identifying the specific skills that will be scored during the try-out; and barring kids who were on a previous travel team from wearing their team jersey to a try-out.

With respect to the independent evaluators, some leagues require them to have certain qualifications. For example, the

2011 travel team rules for Perry Youth Basketball of Canton, Ohio provide that evaluators will be selected by Perry's travel team committee; that evaluators "shall not live in the same household as a player at that tryout;" and that evaluators "cannot be related to any of the players at that tryout." Further, the Perry rules provide that "[t]he coach of a travel team shall not evaluate the players for his or her team."

Some leagues attempt to prevent undeserving coaches' kids from being selected through a travel coach selection process. For example, the Hauppauge (New York) Youth Organization Baseball Travel Program Policies as of April 2012 recommend that only coaches whose kids have "a significant chance of being selected for the Travel Team based on his/her merits" be selected to coach a travel team.

In contrast, the rules for the Perry Youth Basketball Travel Team go in the opposite direction. That team guarantees a spot for the coach's son by a rule that provides: "**Coach's Child**: The head coach's child will automatically make the travel team as long as he participates in the tryout." Maybe Perry has it right. Why fight City Hall? The coach's kid is going to make it anyway, so just go with it.

Other travel team selection rules identify the factors to be considered in selecting a team. Many of them make it clear that a player with a bad attitude or a pain-in-ass parent may not make the team even if he deserves to based on talent alone. For example, the East Meadow (New York) Baseball/Softball Association Rules for Travel Players Selection 2011 provide that "coachability" is to be considered, and that "[i]f a child has shown an inability to follow direction, lacks focus, or has been a behavioral problem, he might not be selected, *even if they are one of the best players in the division.* Conversely, a child who shows a strong willingness to learn and improve, *but is not one of the top players*, might be selected." Further, under the East Meadow rules, a player might not be selected if his parent "has exhibited a lack of sportsmanship towards players, coaches, other parents or umpires."

My favorite all-star team selection rule was passed by the Whitehall Youth Athletic Association ("WYAA") of Whitehall, Ohio. As of April 2012, the baseball league had a rule that, in substance, provided that the "best kids," meaning "good kids" in the Northeast vernacular, should be selected for the all-star team over and above the best players. Specifically, the rule provides that "All-star teams will be selected by each head coach, those players chosen should represent the team, sports-manship, attitude, most improved, are just a few key elements. *The coach should try his/her best to send the best kids, even if this means not sending the all-star or stud player, remember this player represents not only his or her team, but also the WYAA.*"

Ya gotta like that rule if you have WHAA on your schedule. You don't have to worry about facing WHAA's "stud" players. Instead, you get to beat the crap out of a bunch of nice kids who may suck at baseball.

PARENT CODES OF CONDUCT

Parent codes of conduct proliferate youth leagues throughout the United States. The general gist of these rules is that parents should be positive; should not criticize coaches, players or umpires; and realize that the games are all about the kids, not the parents. Given the insane behavior of some parents, these rules are needed. But of the many codes I've read, some stand out.

Let me this time give a positive shout out to the SFPAL. I love the no tolerance referee policy that SFPAL had in its 2006-07 code of conduct. The code emphatically announces, in capital letters, that "SPECTATORS MAY NOT DISAGREE WITH, QUESTION, CRITICIZE THE REFEREE or SPEAK TO THE REFEREE BEFORE, DURING OR AFTER A GAME. THIS RULE APPLIES EVEN IF THE REFEREE MAKES A MISTAKE." The rule correctly recognizes that there is absolutely no reason for a parent in San Francisco, or anywhere else, to be bitching to a referee or umpire about a call. *It's kids sports for God's sake.*

The Half Moon Bay, California Little League 2012 Parent Handbook instructs parents to focus on maintaining their kids' "Emotional Tank," a term that I never heard on a ball field. The handbook implores parents to create a positive environment by "[f]ill[ing] your children's 'Emotional Tank' through praise and positive recognition so they can play their very best." After the game, according to the handbook, parents should "ask your child what he or she thought about the game and then LISTEN, Listening fills Emotional Tanks."

Like many parent codes of conduct, the 2011-12 Champaign Illinois Youth Hoops Handbook prohibits inflammatory criticism of players by parents. But what I like about the Handbook is that it goes beyond a mere general rule on the topic by identifying specific statements that would be inappropriate including: "I can't believe he made another error," "That kid is terrible," and "you need to be tougher."

DISCIPLINING PARENTS

Many leagues also set forth the due process a parent is guaranteed before he/she is disciplined. For example, the San

Francisco Youth Baseball League ("SFYBL") Modified T-Ball Rules 2012 provide that the director of the T-Ball division has direct authority to "suspend…any…spectator…or other person…when that individual's conduct has been determined to be in violation of the SFYBL Rules and/or Philosophy or is detrimental to the best interests of the SFYBL." Under the rules, any sanctioned individual has the right to appeal the penalty imposed by the T-Ball director to the SFYBL Disciplinary Committee and then to the full Baseball Committee.

I should not have been surprised given the infamous Tanya Harding incident, but even youth figure skating organizations have disciplinary procedures in place. As of September 2012, the Jefferson City Missouri Figure Skating Club had a four-step grievance process to be utilized for complaints against parents or others involved with the Club.

First, the complainant must submit a written grievance to the Club President. Second, the grievance is provided to a Conflict Resolution Committee appointed by the President, consisting of the President or Vice President and four board members, who will determine if a hearing is necessary. Third, if required by the Committee, a hearing on the grievance is held. Fourth, a determination by the Committee is made. If the Committee finds the parent or other person guilty of a violation, the Committee "may" recommend a penalty, which will only be implemented if the Club's full board votes in favor of it.

LAWS REGULATING YOUTH SPORTS

Believe it or not, major U.S. cities and small towns have gone as far as to enact real laws that punish parents for bad conduct at youth sports events.

For example, Section 10-138 of the Administrative Code of the City of New York sets forth a model code of conduct for officials, coaches, parents, players, spectators and participants of youth sporting events requiring them to "respect one another;" "respect officials' decisions;" "engage in fair play and abide by all game rules;" "refrain from engaging in taunting of officials, coaches, parents, players, spectators or other participants by means of baiting or ridiculing;" refrain "from verbal and/or profane abuse of officials, coaches, parents, players, spectators or other participants;" and "refrain from threatening physical violence or engaging in any form of violence." Further, that section provides that any parent or other youth sports participant may be banned from attending youth sports events if he or she violates it, and can only resume attendance at them after completing an anger management course.

Another example is Section 9.28.030 of the East Greenwich Township, New Jersey, Code of Ordinances, which sets forth various types of bad behavior for which a parent "shall be banned from attendance at all youth sports events within the Township of East Greenwich for a period of up to twelve (12) months from the date of the incident." Such bad behavior includes "initiat[ing] a fight, scuffle, or any type of verbal or physical abuse or threats of abuse towards any player, coach, official, parents, or spectator;" "enter[ing] the field of play, court, mat or rink during any youth sporting event for the purpose of physically or verbally abusing or confronting coaches, players or officials;" "verbally abus[ing] officials, players or spectators including the use of obscene or profane language or gestures, racial, ethnic or sexual slurs;" or "throw[ing] or caus[ing] to be deposited any object on the field of play, court, mat or rink during any youth sports event." Similar to the New York City law, the East Greenwich Code provides that banned parents can only resume attendance at youth sporting events after they complete an anger management counseling program.

So you parents out there who are poised to jump into the kids sports fray for the first time, just be on notice that there are a load of rules that will regulate your kids' sports activities. They're easy to find – usually right on the league's website. I advise you to check them out. The rules will give you some insight into the minds of the people who run the league. For example, if the league is big on equal playing time, or just winning, the rules should reflect those priorities. For the vast majority of you, the rules won't be a burden whatsoever. They only become critically important when a parent does something really stupid, like threatening a coach or umpire. I assume that most of you are not that dumb.

CHAPTER 11

HANGING WITH KEITH R AT A BALL GAME

So, as you've been reading, I'm into the kids sports thing, which is the only hobby I have time for these days. But when I was a young man, I spent a lot of time on another recreational interest – rock n' roll. My main band was the Rolling Stones. Like most male fans, my favorite Stone was Keith Richards. Keith's rebel lifestyle is now legendary, and I've always been amazed at the way he has thrived despite breaking all the rules.

Given that my adult life has only been about following rules and conforming to societal norms, I never thought that ol' Keith and I could ever have anything in common. But, much to my surprise, Keith ended up living in a Connecticut town very near my town. So, despite the, should I say, different career paths that Keith and I took, somehow we ended up living the same type of suburban life.

Well, maybe not exactly the same. Keith lives in a mansion (I assume) and is a rock star loved by millions of people all over the world. I live in a modest house and I am a lawyer, a profession that has been hated since the beginning of recorded civilization. Keith spent decades of his life partying the nights away while ingesting cocaine, downing bourbon, and smoking dope. I've spent decades of my life burning the midnight oil to write legal briefs while ingesting such dangerous substances as Lipton Tea and Coke. Okay, okay, you're right. Our lives couldn't have been more different. Nevertheless, it can't be denied that we live pretty close to each other.

In fact, I've heard stories of regular folks like me running into Keith around my town in restaurants and shops. Upon hearing these stories, I've wondered what it would be like to bump into Keith at one of the many kids ballgames I attend each year. I thought it would go a little bit like this:

Me: Keith? Keith? I don't believe it, Keith is that you?

Keith: 'Ello

Me: Oh my God, Keith it is you! Do you remember me? 1978, JFK Stadium, about 30 yards from the stage?

Keith: Well?

Me: Remember, I was the only one who didn't stomp on that passed out drunk when you guys opened with *Let It Rock*?

Keith: It's a little hard to see everybody out there man.

Me: I was the one yelling, "Keith, Keith!"

Keith: I'm sorry mate.

Me: You surely must have seen me in Vegas 1994, MGM Grand, mezzanine section?

Keith: No.

Me: Hartford 1981?

Keith: Hey arsehole, if you don't give the "name the concert" rubbish a rest, I'll stand somewhere else.

Me: Sorry Keith.

Keith: Just cool out and you'll be fine

Me: Okay thanks Keith, thanks a lot. So, um, um, why are you here anyway?

Keith: Just catching my friend's kid play.

          [go to the next page]

Me: So, um…um…ah… what's new?

Keith: Nothing much really, just a little grass trouble.

Me: Yeah, I got some brown patches.

Keith: No, I'm talking about weed mate.

Me: Yeah, the weeds can really screw up a lawn.

Keith: [thinking, *this one is a bit daft isn't he*] No man, I'm talking about pot, hooch, marijuana – it's hard to get the shit around here.

Me: Oh....I'm sorry, I can't help you there Keith.

[Keith lights up a cigarette]

Me: Keith! Are you crazy?! You'll get thrown out of the park for smoking. It's a violation of the spectator code of conduct.

Keith: Spectator code of conduct? What, are you bloody kidding me? I've committed felonies in just about every state. I don't care about no bloody spectator code of conduct.

Me: Oh man, you're going to be in trouble. Here comes Regina Lowery, she's the Team Manager. She's one of those PC types.

Keith: Good, bring the bitch over.

Me: Crap, I forgot to bring the team snack. Now you're going to get me in trouble with Regina. Thanks a lot Keith, thanks a lot.

Regina: [*to Keith*] Excuse me sir, did you know that children exposed to secondhand smoke are more likely to experience increased frequency of sinus infections?

Keith: [*while blowing smoke in Regina's face*] The only infection I see around here is you babe.

Regina: [*to Keith*] Well I never! Sir, you're in violation of Section 7 of the Little League Spectator Code, which says that no parent or other spectator may smoke at the field while watching a game.

Keith: [*to Regina*] Hey lady, I'm a Rolling Stone; you know, Jumpin Jack Flash, it's a gas, gas, gas. So piss off.

Regina: [*to Keith*] Jumping jack what? I have no idea what you're talking about. Listen sir, we will not tolerate blatant violations of rules that we have enacted to protect our children.

Regina: [*to me*] And where is the team snack mister? If I don't see some fruit and water from you by the third inning, I'll put you on double concession duty.

Me: [*to Regina*] Now listen Regina, let's be reasonable, that is all Keith and I ask.

Keith: [*to Regina*] You listen to me you crazy bird, if you don't disappear I'm going to bite the alligator off your pretty little pink shirt.

Me: [*Wow, Keith give it to her man, give it to her! Man, I wish I had Keith's balls. What the hell, if Keith can do it, I can do it. What could possibly go wrong?*]

    [*to Regina*] Yeah, Regina why don't you shake that can of yours back to the stands, and let me and my man Keith hang.

[Keith laughs hysterically.]

Regina: [*to Keith and Me*] Oh really, I'll see you men later. Just stay right here.

[Regina walks away in a huff.]

Me: Awesome Keith! Did you see her face when you said that you would bite off her alligator? You rock Keith, you rock.

Keith: Awe that was nothing mate. I once called Margaret Thatcher an "old fart" at some Royal Family event. You were pretty good yourself with that "shake your can" remark. What was your name again?

Me: Jack. [*Wow Keith wants to know **my** name.*]

Keith: Okay Jack, how about a drink? I'm having one.

Me: Sure, what do you have?

Keith: *Jack Daniels* ol' chap.

Me: Well, I don't know Keith, it's a little unusual to drink whiskey at 11:00 am. But if this is how the Stones roll, I'm in.

[30 minutes later]

Me: Gotta love the *Jack Daniels* mate....why am I here again?

Keith: You're watching the kids game, remember?

Me: Oh, yeah...that stuff is pretty strong, what did I have five drinks by now?

Keith: Actually, it was one and a half, but you're already plastered.

Me: I love the headband Keith, where do you get them?

Keith: Special order Jack, but I have an extra one here for you. I'm making you an honorary Stone [*Well look at this, the tool is actually going to put it on*].

Me: Well sure, let me try wearing this thing [*putting it on*].

Keith: [*Smirking*] You look like a real rock and roller man.

Me: Thanks Keith! [*singing into the cup of whiskey*] I can't get no satisfaction, I can't get no girl reaction, but I try and I try and I try...

Keith: Hey Jack give the singing a rest, there's a bloke walking quickly towards us. Do you know him?

Me: Where, oh, that's Donald Browning, the Little League president.

Keith: What's his deal?

Me: He's a stiff, no rocker like us! [*singing*] I know it's only rock n' roll but I like it, like it, yes I do....

Donald: [*to Keith and Me*] Let me introduce myself. I'm Donald Browning, League President.

Keith: So let me get this straight, you're the president of a bunch of little boys?

Donald: No sir, I'm the president of the league.

Keith: It's a bit odd that you like to spend so much time hanging out with little boys, that's all I'm saying Donny boy.

Me: [*in a drunken slur*] Donny likes little boys, Donny likes little boys.

[Keith laughs.]

Donald: That's enough of the nonsense. I came over here to notify you, Mr. Richards and Mr. Malley, that you have been ejected from the field for violating Sections 5, 7 and 9 of the Spectator Code of Conduct, which prohibit smoking, drinking alcohol and negative cheering at a town ball field.

Keith: Rubbish, we never said anything negative.

Me: [*slurring*] Yeah, rubbish!

Donald: Well gentleman, we have the evidence, the Team Manager for this game, Regina Lowery, has made a record of your comments.

Regina: [*stepping into the conversation*] I told you two I'd be back!

Me: [*I hate her.*]

Regina: In the second inning, Mr. Richards yelled, "Hey pitcher, if you don't throw a ball over the plate, I'm going to stick that bat up your arse." In the fourth inning, while his son was at bat, Mr. Malley yelled, "C'mon Ryan nail one, that fat boy can't pitch." Also in the fourth inning, while Mr. Malley's son's team, the Lions, was up 9 to 0, Mr. Malley yelled, C'mon Lions pour it on, these guys suck!" As an aside, in the third inning, Mr. Richards approached Jenny Phillips, who runs the town cheerleading program, and inappropriately asked, "Hey baby, wanna go back to my mansion, do a little blow and get naked?"

Me: C'mon Regina, I wouldn't say anything like that.

Keith: That must have been the other Rolling Stone who lives in town.

Regina: Sorry boys, I have it all on tape [*waiving a cassette tape in the air*].

Me: [*I definitely hate her.*]

Donald: Gentleman, I'd like you to meet Captain Jim Carroll, head of the town police force.

Carroll: Alright boys, you're under arrest for violation of Town Code Sections 8.1 (d), 15.3 (f) and 22.4 (a) (i), which prohibit drinking in public, smoking in a public park, and lewd and lascivious behavior. Put your hands out, we're cuffing you.

Me: [*extending hands out to be cuffed*] Ah shit, this is the last thing I need. Keith, this is all your fault, you made me drink that whiskey.

Keith: [*extending hands out to be cuffed*] Shut up Jack! Take it like a man.

Me: No you shut up Keith! Sir Paul McCartney would have never gotten me into this fix.

Keith: [*lunging towards me*] No you shut up you little wanker.

Carroll: Both of you shut up and get in the cruiser. Sergeant Cameron, take these deviants to the station. It's a wrap boys.

CHAPTER 12

THE LACROSSE SOCIETY

Way back in the day, when I was a kid, Lacrosse was played mostly in the Northeast and Mid-Atlantic states, with the highest concentration of play in select areas of New York and Maryland. But, in recent years, the sport is spreading like wildfire across the rest of the United States. The purpose of this chapter is to give you parents out there who have just discovered lacrosse the low down on the sport, so you can decide if it is a good fit for your kids.

The sport itself is not complicated. The players carry sticks with a little net at the end in which they can carry a little hard rubber ball. The main objective is to score goals by shooting the ball into the goal with the stick. There are ten players on each team including a goalie, and the game is played on a field of about one hundred yards. Offensive players move the ball toward the goal by either running with it in their stick, or passing the ball to a teammate to catch in the net at the top of the stick. Defensive players can take the ball away from offensive players by intercepting passes or by stick or body checks like hockey. The players wear helmets, pads and gloves to protect them from such contact. The sport is fast paced and fun to watch, which is why it is becoming so popular.

That said, the most important thing you should know about lacrosse is that it is much more than just a sport. It is also a culture that has its very own dialect, which is most exemplified by the extraordinarily frequent and admirably perseverant use of the term "dude." Unfortunately, the lacrosse culture took a good kick in the ass from much of the press when the Duke controversy broke, where it was portrayed as an elitist sport dominated by privileged kids who end up working on Wall Street. Admittedly, there is some truth to that portrayal. But it is also true that lacrosse is a much more inclusive sport than it was when I discovered it back in the 1970s. Then, except for parts of New York and Maryland, lacrosse was primarily played by rich kids attending prep schools. Let me tell ya'll how I got the chance to observe this cultural phenomenon, and how the sport has evolved for the better to provide more opportunities for kids today.

During the spring of my freshman year of high school, in 1976, I played on the school's baseball team. However, I knew my future in the sport was limited because I couldn't hit a lick. I saw my first hard slider that year and jumped out of the way like a scared little girl.

So I decided to look for a different sport to play the following spring. I considered tennis, and a sport I had not seen until I reached high school, lacrosse. Of course, from watching Jimmy Connors and Bjorn Borg on TV, I already knew that tennis players wore *very* short white shorts. But, closer to home, my research revealed that being a tennis player at my school was not considered cool, and that as a result, nobody went to their matches.

In contrast, lacrosse had a reputation as a kind of hip, rowdy sport. Laxmen carried sticks they used as weapons, and they were very high in the high school's social hierarchy. Most importantly, I discovered that lacrosse games attracted pretty big crowds, including many of the hot girls in our class. It was a no brainer, I went with lacrosse.

My Long Island high school, St. John the Baptist, was a large co-ed Catholic high school attended by mostly middle class types like me. But, my school also had a strain of rich, preppy kids who had high visibility, and were at the top of the school's social ladder. Among this group of preppies were several lacrosse players. Although I have a clear memory of one of my teammates showing up on the practice field wearing a stereotypically preppy outfit, an Izod shirt, Bermuda shorts and cleats with no socks along with his helmet and pads, most of our players were not preppies.

However, I got a closer look at the prep/lacrosse society when I played lax at Providence College, a small Catholic liberal arts college located in Providence, Rhode Island. Back in those days, PC was not considered a prep haven, like an Amherst College or a Connecticut College. But it has always had a significant prep population within its student body, and can even count a Kennedy among its alumni.

My freshman year was the first year PC had a varsity lacrosse team. So we were terrible. We were so bad that we got the crap beat out of us by the Brown University "B Team." But it was fun to play on a school team for a few more years, and when I met girls in bars I was able to tell them I played a college sport (which got me nowhere I might add).

During my first year at PC, I learned that in New England lacrosse was played almost exclusively at prep schools. For those of you who don't know, prep schools are ridiculously expensive high schools, or even elementary schools, that are designed to prepare kids for college – like Horace Green, the school that Jack Black's character invaded in *School of Rock*. Some of the more well known New England prep schools back in my day were Providence Country Day, Canterbury School, Choate, Fairfield Prep and Port Smith Abbey. So, if you played lacrosse in New England in 1979 through 1983 like I did, you had no choice but to occasionally hang with lacrosse players who went to such prep schools.

The generic male preppy, circa 1980, was easily identified by his uniform like attire comprised of, among other things, Sperry topsiders, LL Bean boots, Izod shirts with turned up collars, Bermuda shorts, turtle necks, Timberland boots and the laughable sweater wrapped around the neck look.

The typical preppy lacrosse players of the day were also partial to such attire, but many of them had an edge that tended to give lacrosse players a bad reputation. Sure, a lot of those preppy laxmen were studious, respectful young men. But many others were crude frat boy partier types with a sense of entitlement, whose typical conversations included excessive use of the term "deutsche bag," stories of their drunken escapades, and explicit tales of the sex they had with the women they "bagged."

Being an ex-lacrosse player myself, I don't want to give you the impression that I was any better behaved than the typical preppy lax player. I wasn't. I just didn't have the country club membership, summer home, trust fund and/or Volvo to cause the sense of entitlement the preppy laxmen had.

Looking back, nothing exemplified lacrosse's place in preppy society more than the outfits worn by the college lacrosse coaches of that era. To this day, I can vividly see some of those guys bundled up on a chilly March afternoon, stomping through the mud in LL Bean rubber boots, donning such ensembles as a turtle neck under an Izod shirt with the collar turned up, under a sweatshirt, and topped off with a team jacket with, of course, the collar turned up.

So yes, back in the day, the lacrosse culture did, in my experience, exude a tangible prep/elitism because the sport was dominated by players who learned to play at prep schools and at public schools located in wealthy towns.

But move forward thirty years or so, to 2013. What is the lax community like these days? Is it as elitist as the press alleged when they had the Duke defendants on the ropes? My son Ryan, who is now 13, played lacrosse from ages 6 to 10. So I've had an opportunity to recently observe the lax community, and I also did a little research on the question. This is what I found.

First, in Connecticut, where I live, the sport is not as exclusive as it once was. When I first moved to Fairfield County in 1997, lax was still mainly played in wealthy towns, like Greenwich and Darien. But now the sport is played in Connecticut where the regular folks live. For example, middle class type towns, such as Norwalk, Brookfield, Newtown, Hamden, Stamford and Southbury, all have high school varsity programs now.

And as I indicated above, the sport is spreading extraordinarily fast across the entire country, not just Connecticut. In fact, *US Lacrosse*, the national governing body of men's and women's lacrosse, has reported the following:

(i)   from 2005 to 2010, high school lacrosse participation grew more than any other sport;

(ii)   as of 2010, governing bodies in 21 states had recognized lacrosse as a high school sport, including states that are far, far away from the traditional hotspots, such as California, Florida and Minnesota; and

(iii)   participation is increasing most at the youth level; more than 360,000 kids played lax in the United States in 2011.

If this national expansion is progressing in the same way it did in Connecticut, where more middle class kids are now part of the lax society, it is a big positive for the sport.

Another change is the emergence of a character known as the *Lax Bro* as the stereotype of a lacrosse player. While the Lax Bro often comes from wealth and attends prep school, his persona appears to be different from the entitled prepster of my day. Many of those guys gave off an aggressive attitude of superiority. In contrast, the Lax Bro is into "chillin," and comes off, at least to me, as a cross between a surfer, a burnout, and a dumb jock.

The *Urban Dictionary* contains many definitions of the Lax Bro, or the analogous "Lax Brah," which are consistent with my characterization of these guys, and reveals that the Lax Bro has expanded lax player jargon far beyond just the classic "dude" overuse. Here's three definitions from *Urban Dictionary* that gave me a chuckle:

1.   "Any male individual who plays (or associates [with] those who play) lacrosse. They wear hats (fitted, trucker, college lax hats), bright colors, and have long hair. Their vocabulary consists of, but is not limited to: word, bro, gnarly, stoked, flow, etc.

Sam: Yo look at those shorts, their soo bro!

Kevin: Yeah, they're almost too bro!

Sam: You can't be too bro, bro!"

2.   "Lax bros are the chilliest of the chill. Everything slides with a lax bro unless it is on the field. Lax bros' schedules usually include some brews, some chicks, and one or two lax sesh's a day. Being a lax bro means that you fully embrace yourself in the culture. It is a life decision to be a lax bro. Lax bro brew of choice Natty... Lax bro shirt of choice lax pinnie...."

3.   "A lax brah is an individual that plays lacrosse and immerses themselves in the culture. This means having lax sesh's, frisbee sesh's (usually with multiple frisbees), or just chillin' in the nice spring weather. Clothing styles var[y] from fresh kicks with high socks, flip-flops, but the best choice is always barefoot. Shorts are worn year round. Flat billed hats are sometimes worn. Hair style is either long or shaved (like a 1 or 2)... A lax brah usually smokes pot and doesn't mind chillin' with some bros....

Lax Brah 1   Dude wanna rip (smoke pot)?

Lax Brah 2   Yaa dude, lemme finish this game of NHL!

Lax Brah 1   Aight motha fucka."

To clarify, *Urban Dictionary* defines "flow" as "[t]he style and essence of a True Lax (lacrosse) Bro. Is usually referred to as long, wavy or curly hair, which can give someone flow, however, flow can also be attained by the equipment and uniform of a player (calf socks, knee length shorts). More importantly flow comes from the style of a player's game; if a player always makes sloppy plays or is a ball hog they are lacking flow, but if a player can make plays and pick corners he has flow. 'Chad has sick flow.'"

Urban Dictionary defines "Sesh" as "[a]n abbreviation for the word session" and "natty" is "slang for the Natural Ice beer brand."

So parents, if your kid has started using terms like "flow" and "sesh" around the house, you should be aware that he may be evolving into a Lax Bro type. While most of the Lax Bro jargon seems pretty harmless to me, I would be concerned if I heard my 12 year old spit out the term "natty" more than once or twice.

One thing I noted during the years that Ryan played lacrosse is that many new lax parents were under the mistaken belief that there are an abundance of full scholarships available to lacrosse players – far more than other college sports. Some of them conveyed this message in an "I can't believe how lucky I am" fashion as if they were among a select few who had discovered this new mystery sport that would somehow provide a gilded path to the Ivy League.

Now folks, I'm all about the American dream. I truly believe that my kids can do or be anything if they work at it – a wealthy entrepreneur, a successful writer or actor, a famous coach, the sky's the limit. But when you're shooting for the stars, you should know the actual obstacles you have to overcome in order to reach them.

As far as lacrosse scholarships go, there are some out there, but there is no gilded path. The maximum amount of lacrosse scholarships that Division I programs can distribute at any one time is 12.6, which must be spilt among the thirty-five to forty players on the team. In practice, this means that even at the top programs, schools like Duke, most lax players are on partial scholarship, and some get zero scholarship money. The scholarship money is even tighter at Division II programs, where a maximum of 10.8 lacrosse scholarships can be issued, and Division III schools cannot offer any athletic scholarships.

On a more positive note, lax, like other sports, can put a kid in a position to obtain academic and need based scholarships and/ or aid. And the ability to play lax on the college level can get a kid admitted into a school with lesser academic credentials than the average accepted student. So parents, if your kid is an athletic and dedicated lacrosse player, by all means he should go for the gold. Just don't buy into the notion that lacrosse provides an easy path to a full athletic scholarship – it ain't true.

In conclusion, looking back over the decades I've followed the lacrosse culture, the sport is really doing great. More kids than ever are playing the game, and they come from a wider socio-economic spectrum than in years past. And you know what? I kinda like the concept of the Lax Bro – a low key dude, who likes to "chill" with his bros while engaging in various types of sesh's both lawful and unlawful – what a life! Although, after interviewing a number of current high school lacrosse players, I think the Lax Bro character is frequently a put on by the kids who convey it. They're playing a role – kinda like the smart, blonde girl who plays dumb to fulfill the image expected of her. I mean, no kid could really be as imbecilic as the stereotypical Lax Bro, could he? Well, at least, I'm hoping that's the case.

However, despite the many changes I've found in the sport, the vestige of the rich prep school lax player is still a part of it. For example, approximately half of the players listed on Duke's 2012 roster played lax at prep schools. And even the names of current players are a dead giveaway. Included within *Inside Lacrosse's* 2012 All-Name Team, which pokes fun at the sport's prep-school stereotype in a self-depreciating way, are the following names, all of which would make any headmaster proud: Baxter Lanius, Brewster Knowlton, Dayton Gilbreath, Wellington Stanwick and Murphy Vandervelde.

So parents, if you want your kid to make it in the lacrosse society, it couldn't hurt to stick him with an eccentric, preppy name. Let me get you started – what do you think of Gilder Cooper Remington-Hemmingway III?

CHAPTER 13

THE DELUSIONAL DAD,
A DAY IN THE LIFE

As I step into Starbucks to pick up my Saturday morning coffee, my mind is focused, focused on Jimmy's big game tonight. Bill Anker, our second baseman's dad, spots me and waves. I return the gesture and approach him to chat about tonight's championship battle. Bill comments, as most of the parents do, about Jimmy's great season. I give him the obligatory thank you, the one I've learned to give to all the parents when they justifiably go on about my son's skills.

As I head over to the line, I forget to ask Bill about his son, or at least make some perfunctory remark about the kid's limited baseball abilities. My wife, Carol, keeps telling me that I must do this, that it is the right thing to do. Of course, I tell her each time that I can't worry about such trivialities because I have a job to do. I'm the General Manager of Jimmy's baseball career. I'm focused like a laser on my goals, er um…I mean Jimmy's goals. I can't be worried about some dad's hurt feelings. Life is tough, he'll get over it.

When I finally make it to the end of the long coffee line, away from Bill and the others, I have a moment to myself. Of course, my mind wanders to the game and Jimmy's opportunity for glory. The big game players rise to the occasion and take center stage on those days. Others cower in fear when the pressure is on. But *Jimmy is a big game player*, he will rise to the occasion. I can see him now, smashing one way past the pitcher and trapping several hot grounders in the infield. Yes, this is going to be a big night for Jimmy, he'll show them what he is made of.

When I finally get my coffee, I head to the car. Oh crap, there's another parent of a kid on Jimmy's team and she's walking directly towards me. What the hell is her name? Her kid is the one who sits down in right field and plays with the dirt. Before I can switch gears and walk the other way, she goes into a rave from afar about some of Jimmy's clouts in our last game. I smile and nod my head. Luckily, she doesn't stop walking. Apparently she's one of those coffee addicts. She goes right past me and says that she'll see me at the game tonight, which is unfortunate because her kid, whatever his name is, hasn't had a hit all damn year.

I dash into the car, before I see somebody else I don't want to talk to. I catch my breath for a second, and my mind starts to wander, as it often does, to Jimmy's great future. His stroke is amazing; he hits to all fields; he has a canon for an arm; he has the type of soft hands that would make Brooks Robinson proud; and he runs like the wind. With these attributes, the college scouts will be coming soon, USC, Arizona St., Florida St. and others. We'll see who offers Jimmy the best package; we'll see who deserves Jimmy's talent. And after that, the big show will be ours.

As I arrive home, I engage Carol, and she confirms, as she always does, why Jimmy is so talented, a true blue chipper. She saw me back in the day, and she knows the story that gives us so much hope for Jimmy, and at the same time brings me so much sadness. Ya see, at the tender age of 13, I was a multi-talented five tool player. I had been a little league star, and my team, Witkowski's Lawnmowers, dominated. I pitched and hit our team to two championships. Man I was good.

I worked so hard preparing for the freshman baseball team tryouts. I worked my body to the bone. I would get up every other morning or so and do at least twenty pushups. Sometimes, I'd even run the around block. Man, that quarter mile was a killer.

Despite all my work I was cut from the team, and it was all my brother Phil's fault. The day before the tryouts, I suffered a serious shoulder injury while wrestling with Phil. The little asswipe attacked me from behind. So I didn't have my best pitching stuff during the tryouts and I could barely swing the bat. The coach never saw the real me, the star that I was. He just cut me man, he just cut me. If it wasn't for Phil, I would have been on that team, and the scouts would have been all over me, just as they will be on Jimmy when he plays high school ball.

Yeah, it's a sad story. But Carol and I will not let the same thing happen to Jimmy. Jimmy doesn't have any brothers or sisters and he never will. We're not going to let some dick face brother like Phil ruin Jimmy's career.

And today is one of those big days, one of those monumental days on which Jimmy can make history for himself, his team and our family. I have no doubt he will come through. Who could forget our opening day victory this year, when Jimmy used his great speed to beat out an infield hit and knock in the winning run in the bottom of the third inning. The shortstop went deep into the hole, jumped high into the air *ala* Ozzie, and rifled it at least halfway to the pitcher's mound. But Jimmy would not be denied, he made it to first safely, yes he did.

As the afternoon proceeds, Carol and I lead Jimmy through his regular pre-game ritual. He will be ready to play, just as he has been for every previous game this season. At 4:00 pm, Jimmy starts his thirty minute stretching regimen, which prevents debilitating hamstring pulls. Then at 4:30, we have batting practice in our backyard, followed by a pregame meal. We head to the ballpark about 5:00 pm and arrive there at 5:15 pm for our 6:00 pm start.

When I step onto the field, I can't believe my eyes. Some asshole is sitting in my spot in the stands, the spot that Carol and I sit in every weekend. What can this dude be thinking? Everybody has a place on this team, and there is a hierarchy that people adhere to. Everybody knows Jimmy is our team's stud player, everybody knows I'm his dad, and everybody knows this is where Carol and I sit. It's our spot, the spot to which the other parents come to rave about Jimmy's latest exploits, and the spot where Carol graciously lies to them by saying such things as "oh no, it was your son's play that saved the day."

I rush over to the stands to give that prick a piece of my mind. He seems a little discombobulated, and barely responds. But soon enough he gets it, he gets who I am, and he slowly moves to another part of the stands. Hey man, nobody screws with me when it comes to Jimmy's career. That guy knows the deal now. It is, for sure, the last time that our left fielder's grandfather will dare to sit in my spot.

Finally, the game starts. The other team, Ralph's Air Conditioners, scores four in the top of the first. Then it is our turn to hit. Under a mandatory league rule, the kids take turns batting at the top of the order. So believe it or not, Jimmy is batting eighth today. I've complained about this ridiculous rule to our league president, Bob Cooney. I mean, can you imagine Reggie Jackson batting eighth in the order so the team's Punch and Judy hitting second baseman gets a chance to bat cleanup? No, of course not. But Cooney wouldn't back down. He's one of those "everybody gets a trophy" guys, whose first priority is "creating an environment where *all* the kids have a good baseball experience." What a loser.

Luckily, even despite Cooney's stupid rule, we score six runs in the bottom of the first. Jimmy, of course, lead the way with a bomb that landed near the first baseman.

In the top of the second, Ralph's scores eight runs because of some sloppy defense by our team. Our second baseman let two balls go through his legs, and our third baseman threw the ball towards first base when he could have just stepped on the bag for a force out. This has been a problem all year. Frankly, a few of the kids on our team just suck. Jimmy did dart over from shortstop to cut off a few balls that were hit to the second baseman, as I told him to do. But, unfortunately, he couldn't get to every ball.

In the bottom of the second, we come back strong with six runs. Jimmy misses the ball on his first two swings. But I knew he would connect on the next swing because he has not struck out a single time this season. True to form, Jimmy belts a grounder to the left side of the infield and speeds toward the first base bag. The third baseman attempts to field the ball after it comes to a stop in front of him. But Jimmy is too fast, he crosses the bag safely before the third baseman can even throw the ball – move over Mr. Jose Reyes, here comes Jimmy!

141

In the top of the third inning, the last inning under league rules, Ralph's comes back with four more runs to take a four run lead. And now we're down to our last licks. If we don't score four runs, the game is over.

We get off to a slow start when Billy Jamison grounds out to first base. Then we come back strong. The next four batters get on with singles, which gives us two runs with runners at first and third. The following batter grounds into a force out at second, but one runner scores leaving a man on first, two out and a 16-15 score in favor of Ralph's.

Scott Slattery steps to the plate. Scott does not have the pop that Jimmy has. I mean he's not going D1 like Jimmy or anything like that, but he's a pretty good little ballplayer. True to form, on the very first pitch, Scott cracks a double down the third base line, and we have runners at second and third, two out.

The crowd goes wild as they see Jimmy striding to the plate. They know that if there is one kid who can take our team to the promised land, to a championship, it is Jimmy. But Jimmy is as calm as can be. With his nerves of steel and talent overload, he is made for moments like this, when only the truly clutch players can rise to the occasion.

Jimmy steps into the box with his right foot and gathers himself, and then the left foot follows to form the stance that we have worked on for years, the very same one that I used to lead Witkowski's Lawnmowers to so many victories. Jimmy's eyes are focused. He's ready to hit.

The crowd is roaring with anticipation as Jimmy takes his first cut. It's a mighty swing, but Jimmy fouls it down the first base line.

The crowd takes a collective deep breath, and Jimmy steps out of the box. Jimmy looks towards me, and I think back to all those hours of batting practice in our back yard, when Jimmy and I would not rest until he got it right, until his stroke was perfect. I look directly at Jimmy and nod my head. I can see it in his eyes, Jimmy knows what to do. This is our time.

Jimmy steps back into the box, and the noise level once again escalates. Jimmy cocks his bat over his shoulder and then begins his mighty swing. Jimmy smashes the ball as hard as I've ever seen – *and it flies off the tee.* It is a ground ball to the second baseman, who attempts to trap it. But he fails to get a glove on the ball and it bounces off his shin.

The fans are screaming as Scotty rounds third and heads toward home with the winning run. The second baseman picks up the ball and throws it as far as he can. But the throw is off line, it lands by the pitcher's mound, and Scotty crosses home plate just after Jimmy crosses first. We win, we win, we win, 17-16, we win!! We are the champions of the Forest Valley, Connecticut 6U T-Ball division!! Move over Mazerowski, move over Gibson, move over Thompson, here comes Jimmy!!

Oh man, let me catch my breath…This is everything I could have hoped for and more. When Jimmy came into this world six years ago, I hoped and prayed that he would live up to my legacy as a ball player, and also live out the dream that Phil robbed from me so many years ago.

Now, after this season, this dream of a season, I have no doubt that Jimmy will keep my legacy alive as he moves forward in his baseball life. He is a special ballplayer. Next year, in the 7 year old league, he will dominate just as he did this year. Yes, there will be one slight rule change. But, c'mon, how hard could hitting a pitched baseball really be? I read the other day that another excellent shortstop, Mr. Derek Jeter, played T-Ball in his New Jersey town before he faced live pitching. So, hey, if it worked for Jeter, it will be a picnic for Jimmy.

CHAPTER 14

SIDELINE CONVERSATION SCENE III: PC LEAGUE PRESIDENT AND HOT MOM

PC Pres: As League President, I am responsible for the intellectual and emotional development of our community.

Hot Mom: [thinking, *OMG, I have to get my roots done!*] Really...

PC Pres: My intention is to create a forum in which our children and their parents can learn to be socially responsible.

Hot Mom: [*I'm so happy for Jennifer A., she's finally found true love*] Really...

PC Pres: Sure, teaching kids the fundamentals of the sport is important, but shouldn't batters think of how the pitcher might feel if he gets an extra base hit?

Hot Mom: [*Yeah Lindsey was right, Terri Dobson did get her boobs done*] Really...

PC Pres: In light of all of this, my goal each and every year is the implementation of league rules and policies that will contribute to the betterment of our culture.

Hot Mom: [*What is this guy blabbing on about anyway?*]

PC Pres: So what would you do to uplift our league culture?

Hot Mom: Um…um…have you considered a mirror in the concession bathroom?

CHAPTER 15

THE MONEY PIT

I realize that one or two of you parents out there may disagree with my extraordinarily well reasoned opinions regarding the kids sports scene. However, there is one aspect of the scene that is undeniable – it is a money pit man, an endless money pit.

When Joe was around 5 or 6, I recall forking over doable amounts for his sports activities – like $75 or $100 to register him for such things as a T-Ball league or a winter basketball clinic. But our sports expenses dramatically increased when Joe was in fourth grade. During Joe's baseball season that year, he had a couple of bad games, and even worse, we saw that a couple of kids may have been more skilled than Joe. Believe me, we didn't take this lying down. Of course, we could have recommended that Joe practice more. But that answer was far, far too Americana, and would have only taught Joe that he has to work his problems out by himself. So instead, we did what any honorable helicopter parent would do, we retained the services of a private pitching and batting instructor at about $60 per session.

Don't get me wrong, I liked the guy a lot. And he must have been doing something right because Joe was a little league all-star. Nevertheless, I often felt a twinge in my spine as I forked over the cash to the instructor. But, unfortunately, those moments of reasonable apprehension did not deter us from the far more onerous kids sports expenses we would incur.

At the end of Joe's fifth grade house basketball season, he was invited to play on an "AAU" basketball team. It felt like such an honor at the time because the coach was the top hoops coach in our town. But the feeling of elation quickly dissipated when the coach advised us that it would cost about $700 to play on the team. Needless to say there was much internal family debate about the proposed basketball expense. We eventually spit out the dough, and that winter/spring/summer of 2006 marked the beginning of our continuous, very substantial "investments" into kids sports activities.

During that period, we coughed up about $3,150 for Joe's various programs, which included pre-season private baseball instruction; baseball cleats/equipment; baseball house league fee; annual "voluntary" little league fundraiser; sports drinks; in-season private baseball instruction; basketball AAU team fee; basketball sneakers/clothes; gas for away baseball and basketball games; baseball all-star team fee; and summer baseball camps.

But this was only a down payment. Since 2006, our sports expenses have gone up exponentially, to our high during August 2011 to August 2012, when we spent approximately $8,015 on sports activities for Joe and Ryan. For Joe, who was a junior in high school during the bulk of this period, the incurred expenses were for, among other things: Babe Ruth fall league fee; sports drinks; gas for travel to away games; baseball trainer fee; high school house basketball league fee; basketball sneakers; pre-season baseball instructor and indoor training facility (to prepare for high school baseball season); high school baseball team participation fee; baseball spikes/equipment; fundraiser for high school baseball team; high school baseball sweatshirt/bag/warm-up jacket; American Legion summer baseball team season fee; American Legion tournament fees; travel expenses for American Legion tournament in Maryland (gas/hotel/meals/tournament t-shirt); college baseball show-case fees; travel to showcases (gas/hotel/meals).

The expenses for Ryan, who was 11-12 years old during this period, were for, among other things: fall house soccer league fee; soccer uniform/equipment; travel basketball fee; basket-ball sneakers/equipment; baseball house league fee; baseball cleats/bat bag/equipment; sports drinks; AAU basketball team fee; gas for away baseball and basketball games; basket-ball summer league fee; baseball all-star team fee; and two sessions of summer basketball camp.

Caroline's main passion these days is acting. But she, neverthe-less, played house basketball and softball during this period at a total cost of about $375. And the acting expenses are no picnic either – they totaled about $2,000. So if you add it all up, our family took a $10,390 hit for all the kids' sports/activities during 2011-12.

Yeah, it's crazy isn't it? But I know parents who are even crazier, who spend thousands more than we do each year on such things as year round private coaching; sleep over sports camps; all-star camps; "elite" travel teams; and higher travel expenses for more frequent and farther trips.

I'm sure you newbies out there are probably asking yourselves, "Do we really need to cough up so much coin just so our kids can play a little ball?" The "experts" in most towns, you know, the private instructors and trainers, pretty much all say yes. Of course, it is no coincidence that they have a financial interest in that "yes" answer.

But let's think about this for a second or two. If the experts are right about the necessity of paid sports training for kids, shouldn't Babe Ruth have been a lousy ball player? As far as I know, when Babe was living at the orphanage, he never had a private hitting or pitching coach; he never had a video made of his swing or pitching delivery that broke them down frame by frame; he never went to any exclusive baseball camps; and he probably didn't even get a new glove and spikes every damn season. Yet somehow the guy had a .343 lifetime batting average, the most home runs per at bat in the history of major league baseball, and the record for the most shutouts in a season by a left handed pitcher.

Given Babe's experience, and the similar experience of thousands of professional athletes who played from the 1920s through the 1970s without their parents paying trainers a fortune, how did it get to this point – where parents are forking over their life savings to vendors to teach their kids how to play sports? How did we become such suckers?

Probably the number one reason is that kids don't engage in free play that much these days. You know, like in the movie *Sandlot*, kids actually got together, played baseball on their own, and developed their skills by repetition.

Kids of my generation also had more opportunities to play pick-up basketball than kids do today. And that was fun, man. You'd go to your local park, and just play some ball. Some days you'd get your ass whipped by older kids or better players, but that was okay. You'd go back a second, third, and fourth time, and sooner or later figure it out. That's how we improved, not by parents putting out big cash to a personal trainer.

The other big reason is the ol' keeping up with the Joneses syndrome. Whether it be the "right" stroller, SUV or SAT prep course, people these days follow the trends with a vengeance. And it's the same deal with kids sports. Parents all over the country are spending serious cash on sports programs that "all the kids are doing." Why? Because there is a feeling out there among parents that if they don't come up with the scratch, their kid won't make it. And no, I'm not talking about the major leagues, I'm talking about such things as a sixth grade travel team.

I'm embarrassed to say that I've done the same damn thing on occasion. I can just hear my stupid internal voice saying, "Oh John Doe is going to that basketball camp, Joe better go too." And then, even worse, I've actually sprung for programs that we really couldn't afford. Argh, it kills me to admit that I've been so spineless. I apologize to you Mr. Ward Cleaver for my lack of character on those occasions.

So all you new sports parents out there who have visions of your little sweet pea playing pro ball or even making the high school team are now on notice – the kids sports thing is friggin' expensive.

Based on what I've lived through, I recommend starting up a kids sports savings account to take the place of the college fund you were planning. Sure, I know some of you out there are thinking that this suggestion is beyond absurd. But not so fast parents, hear me out.

Let's take this step by step. This parenting thing should really be all about the parents shouldn't it? Wasn't it your idea to have your kid? Aren't you the one who spent many sleepless nights rocking your little tike to sleep? Aren't you the one who was puked on when your little angel was sick? Won't you be working your can off for years and years to pay for your kid's food, clothes and housing? Well, don't you deserve some kind of public recognition for all that work? I certainly think you do.

Well, if you spend enough cash to make your kid a star athlete, you'll be a PSP, and get plenty of recognition. Most every time your child has a big game, other parents will come by your spot in the stands, or catch you on the way to the car, to go on about your offspring's many talents. Parents will stop you in the market to rave about your kid's fantastic homer, goal, touchdown or three-pointer. They'll even come to you for advice about such things as which sports camp to go to, and what bat to use. Sure it will be the kid who's actually performing on the field or court, but you will be a bona fide star in the parent community.

I concede that a fat college fund will give your kid a great head start in life. But how will *you* be recognized for achieving the herculean task of getting up enough scratch for that huge expense? Isn't that the question that you should focus on?

Well you better brace yourself for the answer parents – you won't be recognized, and you might as well get used to it right now. The kid will be, well a kid, and won't figure out the magnitude of the financial sacrifices you made until years later. In fact, while you're footing the tuition bills, you won't even get to see the kid much because he or she will be far, far away from you, living on some campus in some other state.

For four long years, you won't get any play whatsoever out of the kid. You know how it is, out of sight, out of mind. And what if the kid could only get into East Nowhere State? You're not going impress anybody by bringing that up at a cocktail party. Oh sure, if the kid goes to some Ivy League school, you can mention it around town, but those kind of comments tend to be forced and just don't come off well.

In contrast, PSP's don't have to work to get recognition out of their kid. When one of their kids runs 65 yards for a touchdown or scores the winning goal in overtime, it is duly noted by the other parents. The PSPs don't have to say a thing, they just have to wait for the post game accolades from the other, less fortunate, parents.

And what is the big payoff from a college education, for the parents that is? Presumably commencement day, when the child receives his or her diploma and moves on into adulthood. But what do parents really get out of those ceremonies anyway? Let's be real, they get jack shit. The ceremony is all about the graduating seniors – it's their day. They walk across the stage to receive their diplomas. Even though the parents funded the stupid college for four long years, they don't get to walk across any stage, get any awards or party with their friends. No, they get stuck making small talk for hours with other parents they never met before. That's no party, that's torture.

And let's be even more real, the damn kids do not move into adulthood upon graduation. If it's a boy, it'll take him a few years to drink his way out of his frat boy lifestyle. And no matter what the gender, the kid will most likely be living home for three or four more years if the job market is anything like the current one.

So while I certainly understand that many of you may stick with your college fund over my creative concept of a kids sports fund, I'm just saying it's an option to be considered.

CHAPTER 16

EARLY SPECIALIZATION SUCKS

A common trend in kids sports these days is "early specialization," where kids as young as 6 or 7 specialize in a single sport. Kids who go that route play the chosen sport all year round, and often have to give up other sports to make time for the chosen one.

For the record, I think early specialization sucks.

Let me show you why, with the below fictional, but true to life, story of Matt and his mom Nancy.

Matt is 8 years old, and has just finished playing his first season of travel soccer. He's a good player, and plays on the "A Team," which is comprised of the best 8 year old players in town. In November, at the end of the season, the president of the town's soccer league holds a meeting with Nancy and the other parents, and tells them about the winter and spring soccer programs. Initially, Nancy doesn't pay much attention to the speech. But then as the meeting is about to conclude, the president hits Nancy with a bomb. He says that it is "highly recommended" that all the boys play in the winter and spring programs, and any kid who doesn't show a "commitment" to soccer may not have a place on the A Team the following fall.

After taking in the president's serious tone, Nancy firmly believes that if Matt wants to play on the A Team the following year, he must play soccer in the winter or spring or both. However, Nancy can't see how Matt can do so because he plays basketball in the winter and baseball in the spring. A few weeks later, the registration period for basketball and winter soccer is closing, and Nancy is not sure what to do. The family has a busy schedule and Nancy can't fit two sports for Matt into it. So Nancy tells Matt that he has to choose either basketball or soccer as his winter sport. By this time, the NBA season has already started, and Matt, who is a big Knicks fan, never misses a game. Given Matt's focus on basketball at that time, it's a no brainer, he chooses basketball over soccer as his winter sport.

As Matt finishes up his basketball season in February, Nancy and Matt are faced with their next sports dilemma – whether Matt should choose baseball or soccer as his spring sport. However, in Matt's mind there is no dilemma at all. Matt has been playing baseball for years, and loves the sport. Nancy thinks the whole idea of focusing only on soccer at age 8 is nuts, but she feels she has to tell Matt what the soccer league president had said the prior November, and she does so. Matt ignores Nancy's soccer comment, reminds her that all his friends play baseball, and declares that he is going to as well.

In late May, a neighbor tells Nancy that tryouts for the fall 9 year old travel soccer season are scheduled for mid-June. Nancy tells Matt about the tryout, and he seems disinterested. About a week later, Nancy reminds Matt of the tryout again, and he ignores her. Nancy presses the issue, and asks Matt if he wants to sign up for the tryout. Matt finally responds, and says that he doesn't want to play soccer anymore. Nancy reminds Matt that he loved playing on the travel soccer team the year before, and she asks what has changed.

Finally, after Nancy continues to pressure Matt about the soccer tryout, he discloses that Jimmy Arnold, the travel team coach's son, told him in school that only kids who played spring soccer would be picked for the A Team. Nancy lies and says that she doesn't believe that a coach would cut one of the best players just because he didn't play soccer in the off-season.

When that doesn't seem to work, Nancy tells Matt that even if he doesn't make the A Team, he'll still get to play travel soccer on the B or C Team. Matt says that he doesn't want to play on any B or C Team, and that he doesn't want to talk about it anymore. Nancy tries to talk Matt into trying out a few days later with the same result. At this point, it's a done deal, Matt does not try out, and never plays organized soccer again. He's out of the game before he even reaches the age of 9.

People, the sad story of Matt and Nancy is playing out in home after home throughout the country. I guess on one hand you could say that kids have to learn to make decisions in life, and Matt made his decision. But that would be missing the point, kids should not be forced to decide whether or not they will "specialize" in a particular sport at the age of 8. That is just stupid. How the hell should any kid know with certainty at that tender age what sport he is going to enjoy playing when he is 14 or 15?

And, in our example, if Matt chose to specialize in soccer and give up basketball and baseball, the result could have been even worse. Let's say Matt played soccer for a few years, got sick of it at the age of 13, and then gave up the sport? At that point, he'd be locked out of playing basketball and baseball on the high school level because he'd be too far behind the other kids. Sure, if he was a really big kid or extraordinarily talented, he'd have a shot at making some high school team. But most kids aren't extraordinarily large or talented, and neither is Matt.

So let's review – how did Matt get into such a tough spot in the first place? The most obvious cause was the league president's demand that the kids on Matt's team specialize in soccer or else.

But the president would have never had the opportunity to screw up if there was no travel team for 8 year olds – that's way too young. As I pointed out in Chapter 6, what tends to happen is that parents who follow the FIFO method are way ahead of the game, and as a result, their kids have advanced skills, fill travel team rosters, and keep them for years to come. The effect of this travel team lock out is that some kids who develop physically at a later age, and become interested in competitive sports at that point, never get a shot to play on a travel team.

Given this phenomenon, the later the travel team is established, the less impact the FIFO method will have on the travel team selection process. For example, if the travel program starts at age 11 instead of 8, that gives kids three more years to try a sport and thrive at it, and it gives laid back parents more time to figure out what the hell a travel team even is. Also, during those three extra years, kids would get a chance to try many sports, and better understand what sports suit them.

Folks, take my word for it, I'm right on this. And the experts agree with me that early specialization sucks. For example, the National Association for Sport and Physical Education ("NASPE") says that kids should not specialize in a sport until they are 15 years old, and that kids who specialize earlier subject themselves to several risks including the risk of burn-out and excessive use injuries. In its 2010 Position Statement entitled "Guidelines for Participation in Youth Programs: Specialization Versus Multiple-Sport Participation," NASPE says:

- Participating regularly in a variety of sports and physical activities yields many documented physical, psychological and social benefits related to both short-term and long-term development and to future participation in both recreational and competitive sports.

- Young people who specialize in a single sport year round encounter several documented risks, because overtraining and excessive time commitment to one activity are disruptive to overall development when a young person is not yet 15 years old and is not able to make informed decisions about life-influencing priorities.

- Positive development is most likely when young people have diverse opportunities to explore and develop a range of physical, psychological and social abilities across multiple activities and sports: some competitive and others focused on adventure and self-mastery under different social and environmental conditions.

- Positive development is seldom achieved when adults encourage specialization by supporting programs with seasons longer than three months and when they verbalize expectations that young people should participate in associated camps and clinics, private lessons and practice throughout much of the year.

- Using intense and specialized sport participation as a strategy to win championships and scholarships, and to create athletic careers often is counterproductive because it frequently causes burnout and undermines overall personal development throughout childhood and adolescence.

- The motivation to achieve excellence is highest when people have experiences in multiple sports and can make informed choices about the sports in which they want to specialize during adolescence.

Based on my review of NASPE's position paper, I have no doubt that NASPE would say that dudes like Matt's soccer league president are shortsighted dolts. Isn't that true NASPE?

Sorry, I digress.

But folks, my main beef with the early specialization thing is that it makes sports so damn complicated for kids and parents. It wasn't always this way. When I was a kid, way back in the day, I played on my baseball team from March into June, my football team from August into November, and my basketball team from November into February. Coaches, parents and kids knew the time of the year that these seasons occurred, and we all planned out our sports year accordingly. We did not have the option of playing organized baseball in the fall or organized basketball in the spring. And we were not pressured to choose one sport over another. It was simple.

Yes, it's true, with that simple system in place, I never became a stud athlete. Indeed, a system has not been devised that could have achieved that feat. However, at least I had fun playing organized sports. In contrast, by the time my son Ryan was 6 years old, he was playing three sports in a single spring season (baseball, lacrosse and soccer). And when Ryan was just 9 years old, he was feeling pressure to specialize in certain sports and give up others. So, based on all I've seen in successive kids sports generations, I'd take my "simple" time over the present ramped up kids sports culture any day.

Unfortunately, however, the good old days of the simple kids sports life are gone forever. So parents, if your kid wants to play competitive sports, you are going to have to play the game to some extent. Depending on how hard core your town's program is, that may mean committing to playing a sport in the off-season now and then, or going to a summer camp recommended by a coach. You'll just have to play the hand you're dealt.

If you have a big beef with the way things are done, I recommend getting involved. If your town's kids sports culture is overly competitive and filled with early specialization zealots, you most likely won't be able to change league policies. But if you coach a travel team and adopt a reasonable approach regarding players' off-season obligations, at least you'll make the experience good for a few kids and their families.

CHAPTER 17

SIDELINE CONVERSATION SCENE IV: EVIL COACH AND MOM OF BENCH PLAYER

Mrs. Halpern: Excuse me Coach, my name is Rita Halpern.

Evil Coach: Hello, how can help you?

Mrs. Halpern: Mikey is my son

Evil Coach: Mikey who?

Mrs. Halpern: Mikey Halpern, he's on your football team.

Evil Coach: What position does he play?

Mrs. Halpern: I believe you call it offensive line.

Evil Coach: Oh wait a minute, I think I remember. Is he kinduva a fat kid?

Mrs. Halpern: Yes, he is a plus-sized young man.

Evil Coach: [thinking, *Oh now I remember this lady, she's not too bright*] Okay Mrs. Halpern, of course I remember Mikey. What a great kid. How can I help you?

Mrs. Halpern: Well, I don't like to complain, but my husband says that Mikey doesn't play that much.

Evil Coach: No, I don't think that is true. Mikey is a big part of our team.

Mrs. Halpern: Oh, but my husband said that Mikey didn't get in for even a single play last game.

Evil Coach: Are you sure about that? I'm looking at my chart here, and it says that #58 was in for 32 plays.

Mrs. Halpern: Oh, but I think Mikey is #63.

Evil Coach: [*Damn, who would have thought this ditz would remember the kid's number.*] Let me check, yes, Mikey is #63. Hmmm I don't see that number. I must have gotten my numbers confused.

Mrs. Halpern: My husband said that the league has a thing called "Minimum Play Requirements" that guarantees that each player plays at least part of every game. Is that true?

Evil Coach: Well, um…ah…ah…Mrs. Halpern, we have one rule that is more important than all the others, which is that the primary purpose of our league is to develop kids into team players. Are you familiar with that concept?

Mrs. Halpern: Well yes, isn't that where each kid does what he can do best to help the team?

Evil Coach: That's right Mrs. Halpern. For example, Sam Bradley has a great arm. So he is being a team player by playing quarterback because our team has the best chance to win when he plays that position.

Mrs. Halpern: Okay, that makes sense.

Evil Coach: And Phillip Martin is our fastest runner, so he plays halfback. That's the player who runs with the ball a lot.

Mrs. Halpern: Oh yes, I've seen Phillip doing that.

Evil Coach: Oh good, you have. So you know that Phillip is being a team player when he plays that position because he is giving our team the best chance to win when he plays it.

Mrs. Halpern: Okay yes, Phillip is such a nice boy to look out for the team like that.

Evil Coach: And the great thing about Mikey is that he is just as much of a team player as Sam and Phillip.

Mrs. Halpern: Oh, he is?

Evil Coach: He sure is. Each and every week in practice Mikey plays in scrimmages against our first team defense during which his team runs the plays we expect our next opponent to run against us.

Mrs. Halpern: Okay.

Evil Coach: And by playing in these scrimmages, Mikey is being a great team player by preparing our first team defense for our next game.

Mrs. Halpern: Wow, I never knew Mikey was doing that. He just loves to help.

Evil Coach: He sure does, and we're very proud of him for his team spirit.

Mrs. Halpern: Oh that is so sweet, thank you. But wouldn't Mikey be helping the team by playing in the games at least once in a while.

Evil Coach: Oh no Mrs. Halpern, that wouldn't help the team at all. We couldn't risk that. If he ever got hurt in a game, he wouldn't be able to attend practices and help prepare the first team defense for our next game. He's simply the best we have at that critical role.

Mrs. Halpern: Wow a critical role for Mikey, that's so nice.

Evil Coach: Yes, and with all the great work Mikey is doing in that critical role, he is one of the top candidates for our "Team Spirit" award.

Mrs. Halpern: Oh my God, an award for Mikey, that would be great.

Evil Coach: Okay Mrs. Halpern, I have to get ready for practice now. Is there anything else I can help you with?

Mrs. Halpern: No Coach. Thank you so much for clearing all of that up. Take care.

Evil Coach: Goodbye Mrs. Halpern [*She bought it; that was genius Coach, pure genius.*]

CHAPTER 18

A FEW RIFFS

Well by now, you've seen that I am a living, breathing font of knowledge on the kids sports scene. I am your guiding light through the tangled webs weaved by the nefarious characters that run your town's youth sports programs. While some men would hoard this special expertise for evil purposes, such as the stacking of a kids hoops team, I am sharing it with you out of kindness. In fact, I'm so generous that in this chapter I'm even offering some opinions on sports that I know very little about. That's just the kind of guy I am – the kind that is not afraid to talk out of his ass. So, as the great Admiral David Glasser Farragut once said, "Damn the torpedoes, full speed ahead!"

Ice Hockey. Never played it, rarely watch it. All I know is that it costs parents a shitload of money, and that kids have to play the sport at crazy hours, like 6:00 am and 10:00 pm, because of limited rink availability. So my recommendation to parents is don't do it. The sport seems like a real pain in the ass. However, if you're somehow forced into it because your spouse is from some cold place like Canada or Minnesota, at least your kid will kick ass in bar fights when he's in college.

Soccer. Never played it, don't know squat about it. But I still ended up coaching Ryan's soccer team a few seasons because not enough dads volunteered. It seems that house leagues have trouble finding coaches because most dads never played the sport. So if any of you dads out there are looking for a chance to break into coaching, soccer could be your ticket. If you take the leap, you'll see it's pretty easy to bullshit your way through a soccer coach gig.

The only thing each team is trying to do is kick the ball in one direction towards and in the other team's goal. I mean really, how hard could that be? "Hey Hans, kick the ball that way." Okay, once in a while you may have to throw in a "spread it out," "run boys," or "good ball Johnny, good ball." That's the entire job, any fool can do it. Since most parents don't know the rules, they won't challenge you as long as your instructions are confidently presented and you follow the minimum play requirements.

In order to fully pull off the con job, however, you must dress the part, which is also easy pickins. "Real" soccer coaches tend to wear Adidas cleats or indoor soccer shoes and a matching sweat suit. So go with that getup. Or, if you don't have the sweat suit, go with a jersey for some European soccer team and shorts. Either way, you'll be in like Flynn.

Assistant Coach, a Great Gig. Has your kid been bugging you to coach his team, but you don't really want to? Are you not much of a risk taker? Then volunteering to be the assistant coach of your kid's team is the answer to your problems. It's a win, win endeavor. If the team wins, you get credit just for showing up. But if the team sucks, the parents will blame the head coach.

And the best thing about the gig is that you can get away with doing practically nothing. For example, if it's baseball, you'll be the first base coach, keep the scorebook or warm up the catcher – all walks in the park. In contrast, the manager will be stuck making real decisions, like picking the batting line-up and calling pitches.

Bottom line, the job is a breeze. So go for it man. If you do, your kid will always remember that you coached his team, and you'll still have plenty of time during those critical parenting years to relax on the couch and channel surf.

CONCLUSION

The conclusion is the part of the book where the author summarizes all that he's said in a profound way.

For weeks I tried to think of a profound conclusion to this book. Something that would crystallize the many groundbreaking points I made throughout it, but I couldn't come up with anything profound.

Unfortunately, I had to conclude that I am not a profound person. This really hurt, and made me feel very, very bad for the thousands of people I have conversed with over the last 51 years.

So I tried to imagine myself as a profound person, so I could imagine what a profound person would say if a profound person were writing a groundbreaking book about T-Ball and Hot Moms n' shit. But as much as I tried to see myself as the generic profound person, I just couldn't come up anything.

Then I thought that it might work if I thought of myself as a specific, real profound person. You know, I would try to think like that dude does and come up with something profound that way. So I imagined I was Morley Safer and imagined what he would say if he were writing a groundbreaking book about T-Ball and Hot Moms n' shit. But I just couldn't imagine what Morley Safer would say about T-Ball and Hot Moms n' shit.

I was at a loss in my quest to draft a meaningful conclusion to my book.

But then it hit me – the conclusion to my book couldn't possibly be profound because it's about T-Ball and Hot Moms n' shit, a subject that could never justify genuine profoundry. So, I logically concluded that even a profoundless person such as me, who is coincidently the author, has the capacity to write the conclusion to this book.

What a relief that was.

MY NOT SO PROFOUND CONCLUSION

My final comments are directed to you Coach Dads out there. Throughout these United States, you're the coaches, assistant coaches, and league officers who run youth sports leagues. It's your show dudes. If you have the right priorities, kids are going to have fond memories of the few years they played organized sports. If you don't, you'll leave many of them with a bad feeling about youth sports that they will keep for the rest of their lives.

So in order to help ya'll – because I'm the kind of guy who likes to help – I'm going to reveal to you the *Jack Malley System for Coaching Youth Sports*. After many years of trial and error, deep thought, analysis, and late night drafting, I was able to piece together my system for the benefit of coaches, kids and families everywhere. It may seem a little complicated at first, but I think you will be able to pick it up. So, without further ado, let me present the *Jack Malley System for Coaching Youth Sports*:

1. It's about the kids, not you;

2. Study your sport so you can actually teach the kids something; and

3. Don't be a win at all costs jerk.

Sincerely,
Jack Malley, Founder
Jack Malley System for Coaching Youth Sports

But wait, you thought the book was (mercifully) over didn't you? Well believe it or not, this book is so damn good that there's even more of it to read after the conclusion, and even after I revealed the true secrets of coaching through the *Jack Malley System for Coaching Youth Sports.*

Following on the very next page, we introduce our brand new comic strip. Move over *Doonesbury*, here comes *Joe Brady, Youth Sports Mogul.*

INTRODUCING JOE BRADY, YOUTH SPORTS MOGUL

He's short, barely 5' 9". He's not a smart man, but that does not matter, for he believes he is and will tell you so. Despite his intelligence deficit, he pushes and bumbles forward during every meeting, ball game and discussion, a politically incorrect bull in a politically correct kids sports china shop. Through his unrelenting persistence, he gets the better of his smarter opponents, who are flummoxed by his far too evident ignorance and decline to call him on it out of Yankee modesty.

He often tells the kids and parents of his imagined athletic prowess, his triumphant days of yore, when he was king, an alleged baseball, football and basketball star. When the listeners of these war stories inquire as to the high school at which he performed these miraculous feats, he tells them it was in Pennsylvania, conveniently far from Rolling Hills, Connecticut, the town he now owns.

He does not stray from the weekend wardrobe that has served him so well for many years. During the baseball and football seasons, he goes with a white "Coach" polo shirt, black Adidas sweat pants, a ball cap and cleats. During basketball season, he simply disregards the hat and replaces the cleats with sneakers. When attending social events, he goes with the classic blue blazer and no sock loafer look favored by country clubbers circa 1975. He wears a cheap toupee that fools no one and provides easy material for his detractors.

He is fond of saying that he teaches his players to be winners. Of course, it doesn't hurt that he unfailingly gets the best players in town on his team by recruiting their fathers to be his assistant coach. He's not much on teaching the nuances of the sports he coaches. Rather, his "coaching" consists primarily of regaling the kids with stories of his amazing sports exploits back in the day; screaming in the faces of his little players when they screw-up; yelling at umpires and referees believing that he can intimidate them because of his "important" status; and dumping as much work as possible on his assistant coaches.

The star of all his teams is the last of his three sons, Chipper. It's no matter that Chipper can barely walk and chew gum at the same time, he is the shortstop, quarterback and point guard of his dad's teams. Any parent who dares to challenge Chipper's ability to play these positions is put down in a manner that would make any mafia Don proud.

While he often tells folks that he takes great pride at being a coach "first," he relishes his power as president of various kids leagues, and wields it in blind ignorance of the rampant political correctness that pervades the kids sports scene. Consistent with this politically incorrect executive style, Joe's teams play to win at all costs, and he gives his players such things as Yodels, Mountain Dew and Red Bull for a team snack.

He is, of course, a lawyer, and president of his county bar where he hobnobs with various local power brokers in a loud back-slapping style. Last but not least, he is married to Kathleen, his wife of twenty years, who idolizes him and waits on him hand and foot, like a slightly smarter, country club version of Edith Bunker. Of course, that doesn't stop him from constantly hitting on hot soccer moms, who revile him and rebuke his blunt advances without fail.

Who is this man? He is Joe Brady, youth sports mogul.

TEAMWORK

DIVERSITY 101

JOE BRADY, THE PHILOSOPHER

UNEQUAL PROTECTION
OF THE LAW

JOE BRADY, YOUTH SPORTS MOGUL™

REFERENCES

AthleticSearch.com, "Problems with Parents? Frank Smoll gives tips on how to handle those parents who cross the line" (August 20, 2012)

HamdenSoccer.com, "The Ten Commandments for Soccer Parents" (August 21, 2012)

AbrahamLincolnOnline.org, Speeches & Writings, Advice to Lawyers "Letter to Isham Reavis on November 5, 1855" (August 21, 2012)

ParentDish.com, "Mayor Steals from Little League" Jennifer Jordan, April 21, 2008 (August 12, 2012)

NCTimes.com, "Ex-President of Vista American Little League Gets Jail for Stealing Funds," Teri Figueroa, May 2, 2007 (August 12, 2012)

ESPN.com, "Baseball Coach Convicted of Two Lesser Counts", September 14, 2006 (August 25, 2012)

Post-Gazette.com, "Jury Convicts T-Ball Coach of Beaning", September 15, 2006 (August 25, 2012)

SI Vault, "Bitter Tee, A Pennsylvania Tee-Ball Coach is Charged with Conspiracy to Injure a Disabled Child", August 8, 2005 (August 25, 2012)

AutismToday.com, "Coach Jailed for Beaning Autistic Player" (August 25, 2012)

SLTrib.com, Monson, "Weighing Compassion, Drive to Win", August 9, 2006 (August 25, 2012)

Reading Eagle, Al McGuire: Profile of Marquette Coach (March 11, 1971)

Newsday.com, "Carneseca Says Jackson is Good Fit for Knicks," Jim Baumbach, May 6, 2008 (August 29, 2012)

ESPN.com, "N.J. Football Coach Arrested for Role in Brawl", October 21, 2006 (August 31, 2012)

Articles.latimes.com, "Antiviolence Leader Goes Anti-antiviolent", November 8, 2001 (August 31, 2012)

HeraldTribune.com, "Sarasota Football Coach Convicted of Battery of Referee", June 20, 2012 (August 31, 2012)

Made in the USA
San Bernardino, CA
14 May 2013